The
NICKLAUS
Way

ALSO BY JOHN ANDRISANI

The Bobby Jones Way

The Hogan Way

The Tiger Woods Way

The
NICKLAUS
Way

*An Analysis of the Unique Techniques
and Strategies of Golf's Leading
Major Championship Winner*

John Andrisani

HarperResource
An Imprint of HarperCollins *Publishers*

I dedicate this book to the millions of golfers who
for so long have idolized Jack Nicklaus, yet never really
understood his swing. Now they will. More importantly, once
they have read The Nicklaus Way, *players who have been*
plagued by the chronic slice shot will know how to
hit the same supercontrolled power fade that made
Nicklaus famous.

THE NICKLAUS WAY. Copyright © 2003 by John Andrisani. All rights reserved. Printed in the United States of America. No part of this book may be used or reproduced in any manner whatsoever without written permission except in the case of brief quotations embodied in critical articles and reviews. For information address HarperCollins Publishers Inc., 10 East 53rd Street, New York, NY 10022.

HarperCollins books may be purchased for educational, business, or sales promotional use. For information please write: Special Markets Department, HarperCollins Publishers Inc., 10 East 53rd Street, New York, NY 10022.

FIRST EDITION

Printed on acid-free paper

Designed by Mary Austin Speaker

Library of Congress Cataloging-in-Publication Data has been applied for.

ISBN 0-06-008885-0

03   04   05   06   07   RRD   10   9   8   7   6   5   4   3   2   1

Contents

Acknowledgments

Writing a book about Jack Nicklaus, golf's leading major championship winner, is not easy. The reason: Nicklaus knows his swing and shot-making game well and has written about it in books, most notably *Golf My Way*. Therefore, taking the challenge head-on to analyze this great golfer's technique and point out secrets of his setup and swing that he was never aware of, or chose not to share, was quite a daring task. Nevertheless, I approached this assignment confidently, based on my experience as a former golf teacher and senior editor of instruction for *GOLF Magazine*. I also knew going in that I had one defense: no player, not even Nicklaus, knows everything about the golf swing.

What also helped me delve into this book so deeply was the support of others, most especially my agent, Scott Waxman of the Scott Waxman Agency in New York. I am also indebted to Matthew Benjamin, my editor at HarperCollins Publishers. It was Matthew, along with feedback from top teachers and other golf industry insiders, that encouraged me to keep looking at the bottom line: *The Nicklaus Way* emphasizes raw swing fundamentals and explores nuances of the Nicklaus method of playing golf, and for this reason allows recreational club-level players like you to hit better shots and lower your handicap.

I'll be honest, one prominent teacher who shall go nameless once said, "Nicklaus created a nation of slicers because golfers copied his leg-drive action on the downswing." Wrong! Golfers slice because they do not understand Nicklaus's swing action and continue to practice the wrong things.

In my search to find out what really makes Nicklaus's technique tick, I learned some of his innermost secrets, thanks to conversations with prominent golf instructors, namely Jim McLean, who was kind enough to write the foreword to this book, David Lee, and Johnny Myers. McLean was instrumental in pinpointing the secret to the Nicklaus setup. Lee was responsible for discovering Nicklaus's secret gravity move on the backswing. Myers is responsible for spotting Nicklaus's unique foot slide, which made his downswing work like clockwork when he was winning the most prestigious golf championships. I am grateful to this trio of teachers and other experts for helping me put together the puzzle of the Nicklaus technique, which sometimes felt like solving the riddle of the Sphinx.

I also thank artist Shu Kuga and photographer Yasuhiro Tanabe. Both these "pros" helped me better relay the Nicklaus instructional message, explaining his superb setup, swing, and strategic game.

Make no mistake: once you are able to form a clear picture of the Nicklaus swing and learn to copy certain vital positions, you'll see how naturally you move back and through the ball. Instead of slicing, you will be able to hit a controlled power fade by making just a few minor corrections.

Foreword

I was honored when friend and renowned golf instruction writer John Andrisani asked me to write this foreword to his new book, *The Nicklaus Way*. John is in a category of his own among golf instruction writers. Obviously, his talents are based on long experience working with the best teachers and tour professionals in the game.

Once before, in 1997, when John wrote *The Tiger Woods Way*, I enjoyed the chance to comment on Tiger's extraordinary power game. Now I've been given the opportunity to write about one of my longtime idols, who has been called Big Jack, the Golden Bear, and just plain Jack. The irony is, there's nothing plain about Nicklaus's game. Like Tiger, he is a pretty fancy guy when it comes to winning major championships, the barometer for judging great golfers.

Nicklaus has entered the winner's circle in major championships a record eighteen times as of this writing, ten more times than Tiger. That should tell you that Nicklaus obviously stands alone in this category. Which is precisely why he was named Player of the Century in 1988, two years after winning his last major, the Masters, at age forty-six.

Nicklaus took over the reins from Arnold Palmer in 1962 after winning the U.S. Open at Oakmont Country Club in Pennsylvania, Palmer's home state. Palmer finished second, and "Arnie's Army" was not pleased to see their hero upstaged. In fact, many members of the gallery booed Nicklaus. But that was all to change once Nicklaus started dominating golf, lost weight to improve his image, and earned the nickname the Golden Bear.

The 1970s were good to Nicklaus as he took control of his game and won the *Sports Illustrated* Athlete of the Decade award. In 1974, he was inducted into the World Golf Hall of Fame. From 1972 to 1976 he was the PGA Tour's Player of the Year. In 1977, he became the first golfer to win three million dollars in one season. In 1978, *Sports Illustrated* presented him with their Sportsman of the Year award.

Nicklaus made his mark in the 1980s too, the highlight being his Masters win mentioned earlier.

During the three aforesaid decades, Nicklaus chalked up a record six Masters titles, five PGA championships, four U.S. Opens, and three British Opens—not to mention numerous runner-up finishes. His success, in my mind, can be attributed to thorough pretournament preparation; an uncanny ability to read lies; a repetitive preswing routine; a very efficient and superpowerful golf swing; a unique ability to hit a variety of creative shots; a superb strategic brain; a very patient on-course attitude; incredible concentration; an extraordinary ability to stay cool when playing under extreme pressure; a desire to improve continuously; a putting stroke, taught to him by Jack Burke Jr., that holds up under pressure because it is so mechanically sound; a highly disciplined practice regiment and ongoing interaction with longtime coach Jack Grout.

Because of this rare combination of attributes, Nicklaus dominated the PGA Tour, winning seventy tournaments since turning pro in 1962. He has also enjoyed great success on the Senior PGA Tour, making only limited appearances but winning ten times since joining the circuit in 1990. Consequently, it's no surprise that many top sportswriters still consider Nicklaus the best golfer to ever play the game.

Nicklaus is an ideal model for golfers who play at all handicap levels, particularly since he has control of the total game, the physical and mental sides. His technique relies on proven fundamentals yet features unique qualities that sets it apart. Moreover, high-handicap golfers who copy Nicklaus's swing technique will experience the joy of curing their slice and hitting shots that find the fairway and green.

In *The Nicklaus Way,* John Andrisani, former senior editor of instruction at *GOLF Magazine,* cites the most important setup and swing fundamentals Nicklaus learned originally from teacher Jack Grout, as a boy, and throughout much of his career as a PGA Tour player. Additionally, Andrisani explains nuances of Nicklaus's game that he never talked about in any of his instructional books or videos, as well as some new swing ideas he learned from other top teachers, including Rick Smith. The ideas presented in this book are proven winners and I'm sure you'll improve by incorporating them into your game.

This book, along with other "Way" series books John has written on Tiger Woods, Ben Hogan, and Bobby Jones, will be a strong edition to your golf library. Golfers, you are bound to gain valuable insights from reading John's analysis of the Nicklaus swing. The new discoveries presented in this book will allow you to hit the ball more powerfully and accurately from point A to point B and shoot scores you previously only dreamed about.

Jim McLean
DORAL GOLF RESORT AND SPA
Miami, Florida

Introduction

On my office wall is a framed copy of the cover to a special commemorative issue of *GOLF Magazine*, circa 1988. The cover line reads, "Player of the Century: A 40-page tribute to Jack Nicklaus."

The issue was a commemoration of the one-hundredth anniversary of the opening of the first country club, St. Andrews in Yonkers, New York, and the beginning of golf in America. George Peper, the editor in chief of *GOLF Magazine*, chose to put Nicklaus on the cover because he felt Nicklaus was the greatest golfer of all time, a level better than Arnold Palmer, Ben Hogan, Sam Snead, Byron Nelson, and other golf heroes, many of which attended a gala affair celebrating the Centennial at New York's Waldorf Astoria Hotel. I attended the celebratory dinner, as at the time I was in my sixth year of a sixteen-year stint at *GOLF Magazine*, as senior editor of instruction.

It wasn't until after the completion of dinner and speeches that I got the opportunity to speak to Nicklaus. I congratulated him and thanked him for what he had written on the aforementioned cover of *GOLF Magazine*, next to an illustration showing his characteristic concentrative stare:

> *To John,*
> *Thanks for the memories.*
> JACK NICKLAUS

I considered it ironic that Nicklaus should thank me, for no other player has given golfers more fond memories of magic moments in major championships than the Golden Bear.

During his lengthy heyday, in the 1960s, 1970s, and 1980s, Nicklaus became the poster boy of clutch golf and class-act sportsmanship. What a golfer, what an ambassador for the game!

I had actually met Nicklaus years before, first in England, in 1981, while writing for the weekly publication *Golf Illustrated,* and then in 1983, at PGA National Golf Club in Palm Beach Gardens, Florida, when Nicklaus was captain of the American Ryder Cup team in their match against Great Britain and Europe.

During the Ryder Cup, I was on an assignment for *GOLF Magazine,* an experience I will never forget. The editor-in-chief sent me to Florida to ask Nicklaus his number-one swing secret. Having formerly taught golf, I thought this was a foolish question, considering the complexities of the swing. Besides, it seemed quite silly to interrupt Nicklaus during such a prestigious event. Still, I did my job.

"There is no one secret," answered Nicklaus, giving me a funny look before turning around and walking away.

To say I felt embarrassed is an understatement. I froze. I was angry too, knowing before I asked the question that one single swing secret could not possibly allow Nicklaus to play a game that even the great Robert Tyre "Bobby" Jones said he was "not familiar with."

I guess it's true that good comes out of bad, because this incident planted a seed in my brain. One day I would find out what makes Nicklaus's technique tick and share my observations with golfers. I do just that in *The Nicklaus Way.*

In the book you are about to read, I talk about the fine points of

Nicklaus's total game, including his ingenious strategic play, as seen through my eyes and those of other golf experts. As you will soon see, I concentrate most on his impeccable setup, technically sound swing, and superb shot-making talent, pointing out aspects of his game that made him play so well for so long.

I'm the first to admit that Nicklaus's magnum opus, *Golf My Way*, is one of the greatest instruction books ever written. Having said that, *The Nicklaus Way* takes golf instruction to the next level by identifying subtle technical points that have never before been revealed. Read the book slowly, so that you understand each point intellectually first. After that, practice each critical movement. Last, blend all of the movements into one flowing motion—just as Jack Nicklaus did when he dominated the world of golf.

1 GOOD HABITS NEVER DIE

*The solid fundamentals Jack Nicklaus learned
from teacher Jack Grout*

One summer day, in 1981, while working as assistant editor of England's *Golf Illustrated* magazine, I was sent on assignment to review a new course opening on the outskirts of London. Quite honestly, I forget the name of the course, but I will never forget the day. Jack Nicklaus, the course architect, was to play an exhibition match with three other top professionals: Severiano Ballesteros from Spain, Isao Aoki from Japan, and Bill Rogers from America.

Once I got the news of the assignment, I could not wait for the exhibition day to arrive in a fortnight's time. Because the event was open only to the press, I looked forward to getting a close-up view of golf's greatest player of all time and pick up some pointers that I could pass on to readers and apply to my own game.

I had seen Nicklaus play before in official tournaments, but my view was almost always hindered by huge galleries and having to stand so far behind the ropes separating the gallery from the players. Therefore, I had never been in a position to analyze Nicklaus's swing. Besides, I had not been writing about instruction back then, so I was not all that interested in technical secrets.

In 1981 my outlook was different. I was very excited about seeing Nicklaus play because I knew I would be able to get close to him on the practice tee and during the round. From these vantage points, I could closely analyze his swing, shot-making game, and strategic play.

On the day of the exhibition, Nicklaus did not let me down. From the time I arrived on the practice tee to meet him and watch him hit warm-up shots, I started gaining insights into technical points of his setup and swing that were never mentioned in his classic book *Golf My Way,* written in 1974. What surprised me most, as I watched Nicklaus select a club, address each shot slowly and surely, hit on-target shots with woods and irons, and analyze the ball's flight, was his intensity. Nicklaus's all-business mindset really impressed me, especially considering that he was playing in a casual event, not warming up for a major championship.

Nicklaus's strong-willed, determined attitude played a major role in his winning ways, particularly during the 1960s and 1970s. But even in his amateur days, winning two U.S. Amateur championships before turning pro, he has been a serious golfer. He has always stuck to a strict work ethic and maintained the same steady and strong competitive spirit. These assets, plus knowing that to promote the best possible swing and shot, you must carefully take the time to correctly line up your body and the clubface, allowed Nicklaus to rise to the top of the golf world and stay there for a very long time.

Even today, though Nicklaus is admittedly entering his career twilight years, every golfer can learn to cut strokes off their score simply by copying this golfing master's preswing steps and address routine—vital fundamentals taught to Nicklaus at an early age by Jack Grout, the golf pro at Scioto Country Club in Columbus, Ohio.

Nicklaus began taking group and private lessons from Grout at age ten, his father and mentor, a member of Scioto, often looking on. Many golfers have heard that Grout was the golf instructor who taught Nicklaus, but few know just how educated Grout was on the intricacies of golf swing technique. That Grout evolved into such a technical whiz had a lot to do with the people he associated himself with. At age twenty, when he became an assistant to his older brother Dick, the pro at the Glen Garden Club in Fort Worth, Texas, he played and conversed with two young golf talents: Byron Nelson and Ben Hogan. As if this were not enough, Grout also learned from pro Henry Picard, when he later worked as Picard's assistant at the Hershey Country Club in Pennsylvania. When you consider that Picard was the man who provided Hogan with golf hints learned from Alex Morrison, *the* teacher of the 1920s and 1930s, and that Hogan dedicated his classic book *Power Golf* to Picard, you can appreciate the wealth of golf knowledge passed on to Nicklaus. If Grout, Hogan, Nelson, Picard, and Morrison were compared to universities, you'd be talking about Nicklaus getting an education from Harvard, Yale, Princeton, Oxford, and Cambridge.

Because Grout had watched great players swing and great teachers teach, by the time he began teaching Nicklaus in 1950, he knew what really was theory and what really was fact regarding golf technique. Grout taught pure fundamentals that Nicklaus followed to

Teacher Jack Grout encouraged young Jack Nicklaus to make a big windup (left) and a powerful downswing action (right).

the letter, a chief reason why Nicklaus became a great player, as well as why you should consider modeling your game after this golfing legend. Grout believed that good fundamentals allow you to better coordinate the movement of the body with the movement of the club. Furthermore, if you set up correctly, you can swing at high speed and still maintain a rhythmic action, returning the clubface to a square impact position consistently. Since young Nicklaus liked to go after the ball, he was more than willing to stick faithfully to the fundamentals of the setup, provided he could give the ball a good old-fashioned whack.

Grout, unlike his fellow teachers, believed that a novice golfer should learn to swing hard initially, then acquire accuracy later. He was sure that a golfer who gets too accuracy-conscious at the outset will rarely be able to hit the ball hard later on. This unique philosophy literally played right into Nicklaus's hands. Once Nicklaus put a golf club in his hands, Grout enjoyed watching his star student wind up his body like a giant spring on the backswing, then swing the club down powerfully into the ball.

Although Grout encouraged Nicklaus to swing with abandon, he tightened the reins when teaching him the vital elements governing the setup: grip, stance, ball position, body alignment, posture, and clubface aim. Nicklaus thanks his lucky stars that Grout was such a tough taskmaster, admitting in his writings that were it not for the early coaching he received, he would never have progressed so rapidly and been so successful. Those early lessons, again, centered on the solid fundamentals. This is why, even today, when you watch Nicklaus set up to the ball, you just know he goes through a checklist involving the technical elements so vital to a good setup, a sound swing, and on-target shot-making. Furthermore, because he practices the positions originally taught to him by Grout over and over again, when he gets on the course, the steps of his preswing routine are repeated practically every time he prepares to hit a shot.

"Nicklaus is a wonder to watch," Seve Ballesteros told me when we collaborated on the book *Natural Golf* and the subject of preswing routine came up. "The way he works his body into the setup and builds a balanced foundation from the feet upward is really a beautiful sight to any avid golfer. His entire preswing process flows as smoothly as a piece by Mozart. If you need a model for your own address procedure, you'd have to look long and hard to find a better one."

I agree with Seve. For an example of unvarying meticulousness in setting up to each shot, nobody beat Nicklaus. This golfing giant proves that an organized fundamentally sound setup enables you to swing the club more proficiently, on the correct path and plane, hit a higher percentage of on-target approach shots, and shoot lower scores. Nicklaus's ability to stick to a strict address routine, during practice, in friendly matches, or in highly competitive, pressure-filled major championship rounds, is the paramount reason he has so many big championships under his belt. No golfer could ever win so many times in America, and abroad, too, without possessing the discipline to train and practice diligently nearly every single day and systematically prepare for every single shot.

From the moment Nicklaus steps up to hit his opening tee shot, he adheres faithfully to the routine he learned as a boy. You should, too, because a preswing routine helps promote a consistent, technically correct swing that in turn produces solid, accurately hit shots. A preswing routine also triggers a feeling of confidence and immediately puts you in a comfort zone. Last but certainly not least, a preswing routine prepares the subconscious mind for the best possible repetition of your intended swinging action. If the brain recognizes exactly what moves the body intends to make, and the precise order in which each will be employed, the swing can do little else but flow correctly and automatically without any conscious direction. Only when something out of the ordinary occurs during the routine, such as extra waggles added to the normal quota, or an increase in the number of times you "milk" the grip end of the club with your hands, does the subconscious mind become perplexed. When this happens, the swing short circuits and bad shots result.

The setup routine, starting prior to address, encompasses several fundamental elements and is so vitally important that Nicklaus claims it represents 90 percent of good shot-making. In *Golf My Way,* he went so far as to say, "There are some good reasons for my being so methodical about my setup. I think it is the single most important maneuver in golf. It is the only aspect of the swing over which you have one hundred percent conscious control. If you set up incorrectly, there's a good chance you'll hit a lousy shot even if you make the greatest swing in the world."

When Nicklaus prepares to hit a shot, any shot, he goes through

Nicklaus has always believed that the setup or starting position determines the type of swing you make. This explains why he always looked comfortably correct at address.

a set preswing routine, literally like clockwork. I timed him during the 1986 Masters, and only once was the length of his routine more than two seconds off his normal time of thirteen seconds. That kind of consistency comes from hard practice and discipline, which is a lesson to all of you. Let's now take a look at the steps of the Nicklaus routine in capsule form before going into each individual element in more detail and telling you how you can apply this data to your own game.

Step 1: He stands behind the ball, staring intently down the fairway.

Step 2: He picks out a specific target.

Step 3: He selects "interim targets" that make it easier for him to aim his body and clubface. Nicklaus has always maintained that he focuses only on a singular interim target spot a few feet ahead of the ball. Recently, however, top teacher Jim Flick discovered one of Nicklaus's true setup secrets.

According to Flick, the reason why Nicklaus turns his head forward and back several times before starting the swing is that he is looking at four intermediate targets: one a few inches in front of the ball, in his peripheral vision, a second twelve to fifteen feet ahead of the first, a third thirty to forty yards down the fairway, and a fourth a foot or so behind the ball, to help him start the club back square to the target.

Step 4: He programs himself to make a correct swing by running a "mental movie" of the ball flying along a specific line and on a specific trajectory. Since Nicklaus normally plays a fade, the ball starts left and gently curves right toward the target. Normally, too, the shot Nicklaus hits is high. He never really got out of the habit of hitting the ball high, having grown up on a Donald Ross–designed course that demands you hit this type of shot in order to land the ball softly on very sloped greens.

Step 5: He steps into the address, right foot first.

Step 6: He sets the clubhead behind the ball, with its face aligned precisely for the type and degree of sidespin he intends to give the shot. Let me stop for a second here and discuss two observations I have made regarding this aspect of the setup.

One secret Nicklaus never mentioned is this: he sets the club down a couple of inches behind the ball, and I believe this little nuance helps promote that smooth, streamlined straight-back takeaway action he is so famous for.

Setting the club down a couple of inches behind the ball, instead of directly behind it, encourages Nicklaus to employ his classic low and slow take-away action.

The second secret: contrary to what he has said over and over, in books and on video, he does not hold the club slightly above the grass. Rather, he rests it very gently on the grass. He does not press the bottom of the club into the grass, as amateurs do. Addressing the ball like Nicklaus will help alleviate tension in your hands and arms and allow you to make a good backswing action. Once you do that, you stand a much better chance of returning the club to a square impact position.

Step 7: He sets his left foot down a few inches farther away from the target line than his right, with the ball positioned opposite the left heel. The open stance helps promote the upright swing desired by Nicklaus. This position will help you clear your hips more easily on the downswing, so you open up a passageway for the arms to swing the club into the back-center portion of the ball. Incidentally, when hitting a driver and most other standard shots, Nicklaus positions the ball off the left heel because that's where the club reaches its low point at impact.

Step 8: He checks that his interlocking grip pressure is light enough to keep his forearms relaxed and promote good feel for the clubhead.

To illustrate how vital Nicklaus thinks grip pressure is, this is the only advice he gave Greg Norman before Norman played the final round of the 1987 British Open: "Grip the club lightly." The advice worked. Norman won the championship.

These few simple words may not allow you to win a major championship, but they sure will allow you to have better feel for the clubhead and swing freely, rather than steer the club into the ball and hit wayward shots.

Step 9: He lets his arms hang freely from his shoulder sockets, as this helps the muscles relax. Moreover, according to renowned teacher Jim McLean, "spaghetti arms" promote an uninhibited accelerated swinging action.

Step 10: He flexes both knees enough to feel liveliness in his feet. "You want that feeling because the swing starts from the ground up," says Tiger Woods's coach, Butch Harmon. The proper knee flex also allows you to establish good posture, as does bending slightly from the ball-and-socket joints of the hips—not the waist.

What Nicklaus never spoke about with regard to posture concerns creating a thirty-degree angle between his legs and the spine in his back. "This starting position ensures that you stand the right distance from the ball, and also enables the body to turn more freely going back and coming down," says former long-drive champion Mike Dunaway.

Step 11: He carefully looks back and forth from ball to target to help him form one last clear picture in his mind of the shot he is about to hit. Vividly imagining the perfect shot induces confidence and promotes a sound swinging action.

Now, as promised, let's look more closely at the technical elements of the Nicklaus setup.

THE GRIP

I still can't figure out why so many instructors teach students to play with the Vardon grip, established by placing the right pinky atop the left forefinger or in the gap between it and the second finger. Even Grout tried to get Nicklaus to hold the club in this fashion, but Nicklaus's right pinky constantly slipped out of position during the swing.

Nicklaus, like the great modern-day player Tiger Woods, prefers the interlocking grip, established by intertwining the right pinky with the left forefinger. This grip gives them a feeling of unity in the hands and a sense of balance, meaning that no one hand wants to take control of the club. The interlock grip also allows Nicklaus, and will allow you, to hold the club more securely at the top of the swing and at impact, too, when you are likely to lose control of the club, open or close the clubface, and hit an off-line shot.

Both Nicklaus and Tiger also promote powerfully accurate shots by holding the club partially in the palm of the left hand

Nicklaus has always believed that the interlock grip, shown here, gives you a
stronger sense of security than the more popular overlap grip. Incidentally,
Tiger Woods agrees, which is why he uses the same grip.

and predominantly in the fingers of the right hand. When you
hold the club like this, the left hand serves as a guide, helping you
return the club squarely into the ball; the right hand provides the
power.

To hold the club like Nicklaus (and Woods), wrap the last three
fingers of your left hand around the club's handle, leaving only

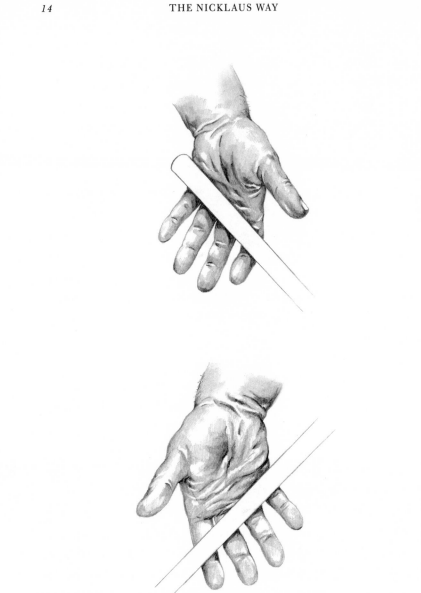

When gripping the handle, follow Nicklaus's example of holding the club more in the palm of your left hand (top) and in the fingers of your right hand (bottom).

your thumb and forefinger off the club. Next, lower your left thumb, allowing it to pinch the right center portion of the grip. Next, simply work the pinky of your right hand between the first and second fingers of your left hand. Lower your right thumb, so that its right side rests on the left center portion of the grip. Next, press the pad of your right hand against your left thumb. Finally, jockey your fingers around until you feel a unified sensation in both hands, then squeeze the club's handle a little more firmly with the last two fingers of your left hand and the middle two fingers of your right.

Whereas almost all golf professionals complete the grip by pressing the inside tip of their right thumb against the inside tip of their right forefinger, I noticed a nuance or secret of the Nicklaus grip when watching this master swinger set up to the ball. He lets his right forefinger hook under the club's handle in such a way that he establishes a noticeable gap between the aforementioned finger and his right thumb. This aspect of Nicklaus's grip has never been discussed, though I believe that during his heyday it was one of his best-kept secrets.

In analyzing this personal idiosyncrasy, I believe that by not pressing the right thumb and right forefinger against each other, he alleviates the possibility of the right hand overpowering the left hand through impact, closing the clubface, and hitting a hook. Nicklaus preferred that the clubface be slightly open at impact, especially when hitting a more exaggerated left-to-right shot.

If you've got a hooking problem, or simply want to play the same controlled fade shot as Nicklaus, try putting some air between your right thumb and right forefinger.

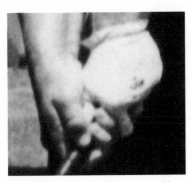

Nicklaus's unique right forefinger position was one of his secrets to hitting his classic left-to-right power fade.

STANCE

When Nicklaus first emerged onto the professional golf scene in the early 1960s, he stuck out like a sore thumb on the practice tee, and not just because he was the biggest and blondest young guy in the lineup of players hitting balls. One reason Nicklaus caught the attention of other players was because he took an open stance rather than the more common closed stance. He also set his right foot perpendicular to the target line, rather than flare it out about twenty-five degrees as other pros did. This starting position—still the same today—helps Nicklaus swing the club on an upright plane and hit a fade. Other players of his day, namely Palmer, preferred to hit a draw because it provided them with more distance due to additional roll resulting from overspin on the ball. Today, more players prefer to hit a controlled fade, so they set up just like Jack.

Yet another difference between Nicklaus's stance and that of other pros was its width. When he was playing his best golf, Nicklaus's driver stance was a few inches wider than shoulder width apart, much like Tiger's is today.

"One advantage of the extra-wide stance is that it allows you to

Nicklaus has always played from an open stance because this position helps promote a highly controlled fade shot.

extend the club back low for a longer period of time, in the take-away and at the halfway point of the backswing," says Rick Grayson, one of America's top teachers. "Therefore, it helps you create the fullest possible swing arc, which was something else Grout believed in. The wider the swing arc, the more clubhead speed you generate, and the farther you will hit the ball."

"A second advantage of the extra-wide stance is that it allows you to make a powerful swing while still keeping your weight on the inside of your right heel during the backswing and on the inside of your left heel during the downswing," says Minnesota-based golf instructor Gerald McCullagh. "Playing from the insides of the feet allows Nicklaus to stay balanced and maximize control of the fast-moving club."

According to Bill Davis, one of golf's most savvy instructors, "A third advantage of the extra-wide stance is that it allows you to increase the flat spot in your swing. Swinging the club through the ball in a more streamlined fashion, instead of employing a faulty chopping action through impact, allows you to keep the club on the ball a split second longer. As a result, you hit the ball longer and straighter."

Make no mistake; the Nicklaus stance is better for you, as illustrated by these additional words of wisdom by two golfing icons, Ken Venturi and Jim McLean. "The most powerfully accurate drivers in the game place the feet much wider than shoulder width apart," says former CBS golf analyst Venturi. This comment is more creditable when you consider that Venturi, the 1960 U.S. Open champion, played out of a wide base and hit the ball a country mile.

Jim McLean, who has studied Nicklaus for years, cites other advantages of the Nicklaus-type stance: "The wide stance provides a low center of gravity for stability, and allows a player to push the feet off the ground more powerfully. If you had one chance to deliver your hardest punch and win the heavyweight crown, you would instinctively spread your feet. When a baseball slugger connects with power, it's because he or she has stepped forward and hit from a broad base."

BALL POSITION

More professional players and top amateurs position the ball opposite the left heel when driving, then move it back gradually in their stance as the clubs get shorter and more lofted. Nicklaus, on the other hand, plays every standard shot—driver, fairway wood, long iron, middle iron, short iron—off the left heel. Following Nicklaus's

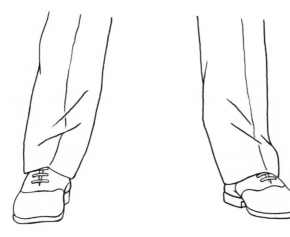

Nicklaus positions the ball directly opposite the left heel to play all standard shots.

Nicklaus's open body alignment allowed him to hit the ball more powerfully than any other golfer, when he was a college player (left) and when he exploded onto the PGA Tour scene (right).

example will give you more time to clear your hips on the downswing, thereby allowing you to hit the ball more crisply, more often.

BODY ALIGNMENT

This feature of Nicklaus's setup was also unorthodox compared to his contemporaries who played the tour during the 1960s and 1970s. He set his feet, knees, hips, and shoulders left of the target line, rather than in a square or closed position. Nicklaus still usually prefers this alignment position because it promotes an upright

swing, allows him to move more freely through the ball in the impact zone, and helps him hit controlled fade shots.

POSTURE

Nicklaus is the one player whose address comes closest to matching his impact position. This, in fact, is another of his secrets to success.

To increase your chances of dropping the club into the perfect hitting slot on the downswing, and propel the ball toward the target, follow Nicklaus's example and

    1. Tilt your chin away from the target, so your head is behind the ball.

2. Let your left arm be an extension of the clubshaft, with
   the two forming a straight line.
3. Let your left shoulder be higher than your right.
4. Let your left hand be slightly ahead of the ball.

Posture seems inconsequential to many recreational golfers, who unfortunately choose to do their own thing at address. The typical player stands very erect or stoops over. This is a big mistake, because as Nicklaus says himself in the book *Jack Nicklaus's Lesson Tee,* "Your posture at address is very important because it controls both the plane of your swing and your balance."

CLUBFACE AIM

Nicklaus aims the clubface directly at the target but right of where he aims the body. This position helps him hit a fade, executed by swinging across his body line. I think if you try fading the ball this way, rather than taking a weak grip and swinging on an exaggerated out-to-in plane, you'll feel more comfortable and be a more consistent player.

As you read about Nicklaus's setup, you can see that it is fundamentally sound, but it also includes some very personal elements that you should consider experimenting with. Whichever way you choose to go, either strictly by the book or allowing yourself some leeway, make sure to practice hard. I am not saying that you have to go so far as to set up a miniature driving range in your basement, as Nicklaus did so that he could work on his swing on cold or rainy days or in the evening. I am saying that if you really are serious about improving your golf game, you had better be willing to sacrifice some time on the course for some time on the driving range.

That, my friends, does not just mean beating balls. It means spending time checking your setup in a mirror. It means allowing yourself to be videotaped, so that you spot faults in your technique and correct them before they ruin your game. It also means practicing with a variety of clubs and taking time before each shot to carefully go through a routine—just as Nicklaus does every single time he prepares to hit the ball.

You don't need to build a practice facility in your basement, like Nicklaus did, but you must learn to sacrifice playing time for practice time if you want to become good at golf.

Nicklaus's Nuances

◆ Nicklaus was taught to learn how to hit the ball powerfully first, and worry about accuracy later. This is good advice for any beginner, particularly a junior golfer.

◆ Before swinging, Nicklaus stands behind the ball and lets a movie storyboard of the perfect shot play on the big screen of his mind. This same mental imagery will encourage you to hit good shots.

◆ When setting up, Nicklaus uses four target spots to help him line up. You may want to consider using at least one "interim target," since it will help ensure correct body and clubface alignment.

◆ At address, Nicklaus sets the club down a few inches behind the ball, not directly behind it. This tip will help promote the desired low take-away action.

◆ Nicklaus lets his right forefinger hook under the club's handle, so there's a noticeable gap between the tip of the aforementioned finger and the right thumb. This unique hold will prevent your right hand from controlling the downswing—a cause of so many wayward shots.

◆ Nicklaus plays all standard shots off his left heel. To be a more consistent shot-maker, follow his example.

◆ In playing the fade, Nicklaus aims his body left of target, and aims the clubface at the target, then swings normally. Try this technique, rather than weakening your grip and swinging on an exaggerated out-to-in path, as so many high handicappers do.

2 IN THE SWING

*The secrets to Nicklaus's unique backswing and
downswing actions*

The two paramount reasons why Jack Nicklaus has captured seven more major championships than his closest rival, the late Walter Hagen, and ten more than Tiger Woods, is that he possesses a clear image of the backswing and downswing in his head, plus an ability to physically swing according to that mental plan.

Something else that has allowed Nicklaus to be so successful is not delving too deeply into technique. After taking serious instruction from Grout during his younger days and early pro days, he pretty much just reported back to him for tune-up lessons. Tiger, on the other hand, shows a certain degree of insecurity about understanding his swing technique, evidenced by his close and almost obsessive relationship with former teacher Butch Harmon. Harmon told me himself that when not on the road with Tiger, he frequently talked on the telephone with his star student. They also exchanged videotapes, containing either swings of past great players or Tiger's swing, with comments from Butch.

Nicklaus never needed this kind of constant attention. That's because he had a better understanding of his swing than Tiger and felt more secure about it. Therefore, he entered each and every tournament feeling superconfident. Tiger does too, yet when something goes wrong with his swing, he seems to need more time to correct it than Nicklaus did.

When Nicklaus played in the 1960s, 1970s, and 1980s, he paid close attention to a few swing principles, rather than get so wrapped up in technique that he experienced "paralysis by analysis." The majority of these swing basics were taught to Nicklaus by Grout, while the others Nicklaus figured out himself through trial and error.

From Grout, he learned that

1. The head must stay still during the backswing and downswing.
2. The key to maintaining good balance is footwork—the correct rolling of the ankles to promote a solid back-and-through weight-shift action.
3. The key to creating maximum power at impact is to create the widest possible swing arc through extension.

On his own, Nicklaus learned that the best ways to consistently keep the swing under control and return the clubface squarely and powerfully into the ball at impact involved

1. Using a forward press action to trigger the swing
2. Taking the club away very slowly and gradually, in one piece, to build up speed until impact, when power is released fully

Footwork is one of Nicklaus's less talked about swing secrets, yet when he was a young boy, Jack Grout taught him how to use his feet to control the tempo, timing, and rhythm of the swing.

3. Swinging the club on an upright plane rather than a flat plane
4. Purposely letting the right elbow move outward from the body to promote the desired upright plane
5. Letting the swinging weight of the clubhead cause the wrists to hinge as the club is swung to the top
6. Replanting the left foot and driving the legs toward the target to trigger the downswing

7. Striving for a full finish to promote acceleration through
   the ball

Now that I have given you a quick breakdown of Nicklaus's master keys, you should be ready for a more detailed explanation of these vital elements. I will also cover other Nicklaus swing secrets, both orthodox and unorthodox, based on my in-depth analysis of this great player's technique.

As you go through the instructional text, let the illustrations of Nicklaus swinging guide you to form a vivid mental picture of what

Throughout his career, Nicklaus has believed that one sure way to promote clubhead acceleration in the hitting area is to strive for a full finish position.

writer Ken Bowden called "the epitome of the modern method and a superb model for every golfer" in the book *The Masters of Golf.*

THE BACKSWING

Nicklaus realized early on in his golf career that it is almost impossible to start the swing from a static setup position without jerking the club away and disrupting the tempo, timing, and rhythm of his swing. He figured out that for the address or starting position to flow smoothly into the backswing, he had to move the club slightly toward the target. This forward press action, made famous by such pros as Bobby Jones and Ben Hogan, allowed Nicklaus to make a smooth take-away a necessary ingredient to promoting a rhythmic backswing.

The take-away is one of the most critical stages of the swinging action. If this move is incorrect or overly fast, there is little chance that you will be able to swing back on track and achieve your ultimate goal: square and solid clubface-to-ball contact at impact. The only way to bail out a bad start is to reroute the club back along the proper path and plane by jerking it. Do that, though, and you'll destroy your natural tempo and rhythm and at best hit a shot that finishes several yards off line. Even an experienced player like Nicklaus, who possesses the talent to feel an early error, can rarely correct it in midstream and hit the shot as planned. The backswing takes around one and one half seconds to complete, while the downswing merely one-fifth of a second, so your reflexes can't react quickly enough to redirect a faulty start.

If you watch Nicklaus in action, particularly old video footage showing his swing, you'll notice that his take-away action is superdeliberate—SLOW. Making a slow, smooth start is the only proven way to ensure a strong coiling action of the body and a proper weight-shift action on the backswing—two keys to powerfully accurate hits. In the words of Sandy Lyle, who was paired with Nicklaus on the final day at the Masters in 1986, when Nicklaus came from behind to win, "A waltz is better than a quick step." The bottom line: take it slow at the start, and you'll establish good overall tempo, a must for putting the clubface squarely on the ball. Contrarily, employ a fast take-away action, and you'll probably be talking to yourself after a few bad shots.

Nicklaus knew growing up that there are various ways to start the club back. He learned this from observing top players, just as Tiger has done. For example, some players push off the ball of the left foot, while others rotate the left shoulder under the chin, or turn the left knee inward, and some use such triggers as turning the right hip clockwise or gently pulling the club back with the right hand.

Nicklaus chose none of these backswing triggers to model his take-away after. Instead, he figured out that by synchronizing the movement of the left shoulder, left arm, clubshaft, left hip, and left knee away from the ball, he could promote a dependable backswing that would hold up under pressure and repeat itself again and again.

"This one-piece take-away also helps Nicklaus create a tremendously wide arc on his backswing," says David Leadbetter, one of the most respected teachers in the golf industry.

One mistake the average country club player makes in the take-away is to pull the club away inside the target line. Consequently, the player loses power because the club swings so far to the inside that nine out of ten times it is delivered into impact with its face pointing well left or right of target.

Nicklaus *pushes* the club away, which is "much more fluid, natural, and powerful than a pulling action," according to top teacher Peter Croker.

Nicklaus also discovered that if you set up to the ball correctly, keep your wrists firm, and coil the shoulders in a clockwise direction, the club will correctly start back along the target line, then gradually swing to the inside automatically.

To prove that the rotation of the shoulders promotes an inside take-away, try this experiment: Set up to a wall, resting the toe end of the clubhead flush to the backboard or molding. Then, after triggering the swing by gently pushing the club straight back for six inches or so, begin turning your shoulders clockwise without excessively twisting your lower body or manipulating the club in any fashion with your hands. You will discover that there simply is no other place the clubhead can swing but away from the wall, which, on the golf course, means to the inside of the target line.

Nicklaus never wants his hands to do anything else but hold on to the club. He believes that golfers will play much better golf if they swing the club through the hands and not with them. Maybe this sounds to you like semantics; talk to anyone who understands the game, however, and you'll discover that it is a fact.

When Nicklaus hits his bread-and-butter fade shot, the club swings straight back and low to the ground for about twelve inches before moving to the inside. He employs this low inside take-away for a couple of reasons. First, a low take-away is the first step to good extension on the backswing and a wide and powerful arc of swing. Second, the lower the club moves at the start of the swing, the better the chance of it moving low through impact. Power hitter John Daly, whose idol is Jack Nicklaus, proves this. Daly told me that he actu-

Gradually, on the backswing, the club moves from a straight back position (left) to a position well inside the target line (right).

ally drags the club back so low that the bottom of the club, or "sole," grazes the grass for about the first eighteen inches of the swing. He also told me that if he were to pick the club up quickly in the takeaway, he'd create a narrow arc of swing and chop down on the ball in the impact zone. By the way, try looking at early photographs of Nicklaus; his clubhead actually brushed the ground, too.

It is not surprising that Nicklaus was the longest and most accurate driver of his day, considering the fullness of his arc. Grout taught Nicklaus that the width of the swing arc is directly related to

the radius formed by the left arm and the clubshaft. Further, the radius is like a spoke in a wheel, in that it must remain stable for maximum acceleration and efficiency.

Nicklaus's extra-wide stance helps him establish a wide arc of swing, as does his ability to control the swing with the strong muscles of the arms and shoulders. Through experimentation in practice, Nicklaus discovered that letting the hands take control of the swing can cause the wrists to hinge too early, the left arm–club radius to break down, the swing arc to narrow and weaken, and power to be drained from the swing.

As the take-away process continues, with the shoulders and hips turning clockwise, Nicklaus's hands swing past the right side of his body while both arms stay fairly taut and the wrists remain locked. This delayed wrist-hinge is what allows Nicklaus to maintain the swing radius he established at address and in earlier stages of the take-away, and thus remains one of his secrets to creating the widest and most powerful swing arc.

If you were to take a reading of the Nicklaus backswing, once his hands reach waist level, this is what you would see:

1. The clubshaft is parallel to the body line.

Nicklaus delays the hinging action of the wrists early in the backswing to help create a wide and powerful swing arc.

2. Nicklaus's head is still.

3. Nicklaus's left kneecap is even with the ball.

4. Nicklaus's left shoulder is nearly under his chin.

5. Nicklaus's right leg is braced, with approximately 70 percent of his body weight on his right foot.

6. The back of Nicklaus's left hand is virtually parallel to his body line.

As long as Nicklaus just keeps swinging the club on the proper path and plane, again with no hand manipulation, he will maintain the straight-line relationship formed by the back of his left hand and the back of his left forearm. There will be no concavity or convexity at the back of his left hand. In teaching terms, his left wrist is said to be "flat," not "cupped."

Nicklaus knows his take-away is over when he feels weight shift or roll from his left foot to his right foot, so much so that he feels the left heel want to lift off the ground. My advice is to let the heel come off the turf, because it will increase your ability to turn your body fully and create power. "The old-school teachers like Percy Boomer and the great Scottish pros want the left heel to come up in the backswing and return to the ground at the start of the downswing," said the late great golf instructor Harvey Penick in *Harvey Penick's Little Red Book*. "I think the reason Jack Nicklaus has such good control at the top is that he lets that left heel come up, releasing a full action."

Nicklaus's left heel rises well off the ground, which is probably the reason he is still able to make such a full coiling action without putting strain on his back. Tiger is a much more flat-footed player, and that is the reason I believe he sometimes suffers from severe backache.

It's important to emphasize here that most of the left foot comes off the ground naturally. Don't ever consciously lift your left heel off the ground, or else you'll tend to slide your body to the right or "sway," shift too much weight to the outside of your right foot, lose your balance, and throw off the timing of your swing.

According to David Lee, one of the nation's top teachers and the innovator of the Gravity Golf teaching method, Nicklaus shifts weight back to his left side as he completes his backswing turn. This action, which Lee considers a secret move of Nicklaus's, is very similar to the one used by a baseball pitcher. The fall from the mound onto the left leg creates pivotal speed without increased effort. Without the occurrence of this "counterfall" action, power leaks from the swing. So learn to groove the proper action by following Lee's recommendation to hit shots standing on only your left leg.

According to Lee, the gravity swing sets up maximum leverage in the body through a totally different system of timing. It has generally been taught that the club swings back while the weight moves to the right side, and the club swings forward while the weight moves back to the left side. In the gravity swing, the weight moves to the right and returns to the left side while the club is still going back. Even though there is a definite flow of weight to the right side, the player's center of gravity remains over the left side through a falling action. Gravity makes this move for you, not muscular effort, hence the term *gravity golf*. The weight falls back into the left thigh just before the hands reach the top of the backswing. The left thigh reacts to the weight being dropped into it and makes a turning or clearing motion. It is this "reaction hip turn" that pulls the arms, hands, and club down and through the ball. The result is a swing with all the leverage (power) of which your body is capable, but with the least amount of effort. The shot you hit starts flying low, then soars to a great height, just like the ones Nicklaus hit so many times during major championships.

Although many teachers criticized Lee for advocating such a move, Lee knew that he was on to something, having received a letter from Jack Nicklaus following a lesson he gave him. Nicklaus wrote, "It seems to me that you have come up with a new approach to teaching that is extremely valid. I believe the teaching method you have developed could be applied with great benefit to all levels of golfers. It certainly has revealed things to me about my own swing that I had not previously been aware of, and that, I am sure, will help me personally with my game." This letter shows that Nicklaus discovered one of his hidden secrets that he previously was unaware of. This secret has never been shared with golfers in any other book before now.

There's no sudden jerk with the hands to move the club upward. Essentially, along with the gravity move, it is the synchronized and coordinated turning actions by both hips and both shoulders that cause the club to swing up. To further enhance power and complement his wide-arc swing, Nicklaus keeps his head still as he coils his body, knowing what Ben Hogan knew: a steady head helps you create resistance or torque between the upper and lower body. Thus, when you swing to the top, you will feel like a catapult ready to spring back, in this case in the direction of the target.

Incidentally, the reason Nicklaus was able to keep his head still, and as a result build powerful torque and generate high clubhead speed, had to do with his early training. Grout was so strict about

Nicklaus coils his hips and shoulders to help boost the club upward, so that no manipulation is required from the hands.

the steady head position that he grabbed Nicklaus's hair when he stood at address. If Nicklaus moved his head too much as he swung, he'd feel pain. I really don't recommend this way of learning. Just concentrate on keeping your head fairly still during the swing, and you'll be all right.

In swinging to the top, Nicklaus lets his right elbow fly to promote an upright plane that he believes is better than a flat plane. What I mean by "fly" is this: the right elbow is more up than in the tucked-in position that many golf coaches advocate. Instead of pointing down, the right elbow points outward.

Nicklaus's unorthodox flying-right-elbow position (top) further ensures an upright plane of swing (bottom).

Two modern-day power hitters and major championship winners who copied this unorthodox right-elbow move, years after Nicklaus was criticized for drastically going against the book, are John Daly and Fred Couples. Because I think the flying right elbow would benefit recreational golfers, I can't understand why so many of today's top teachers advise students to keep the right elbow so close to their body that they are able to hold a handkerchief under the right armpit while swinging the club back to the top.

The flying right elbow is the source of a lot of controversy in the golf swing. It's been stated many times by teachers writing articles in golf magazines that a winging right elbow means that the swing is not on plane, that it's too upright. Well, this is exactly the plane of swing that made Nicklaus such a good ball-striker and consistent player who hit a lot of fairways and greens. "An upright plane gives the golfer his best chance of swinging the club along the target line at impact," said Nicklaus in *Golf My Way*.

The other advantage of the upright plane, one Nicklaus overlooked in his writings, is that it makes you a more effective player when hitting recovery shots from the rough. As accurate as Nicklaus was, his ball sometimes landed in the rough, especially at the British Open, where typically the winds blow the ball off line, or at the U.S. Open, where the fairways are supernarrow.

In the rough, when your club approaches the ball from this more upright angle, there is less chance that long grass will wrap around the hosel of the club and slow its momentum, muffling the shot. Also, with the upright swing, less grass intervenes between the club and ball at impact, so you are able to impart more backspin to your shots.

While he looks to swing on an upright plane, it's obvious that Nicklaus also goes to great lengths to maintain a wide arc by reaching for the sky with his hands.

If you swing the club on the correct plane, it does not matter if you take the club back to the three-quarter position (this page), as Nicklaus did when he first started playing the PGA Tour, or the parallel position (next page), as he did later on in his career.

To some degree your build determines the nature of the swing plane. The tall player who stands close to the ball at address can naturally make a more upright backswing than the shorter player. Nevertheless, bear in mind that Nicklaus, who is under six feet tall, had no trouble making a very upright swing, so it definitely can be done. Moreover, it should be done, for the reasons already cited and for this one too: when you deliver the clubhead from a more upright angle, like Nicklaus, it doesn't matter as much whether

your ball position is perfect. This is because the clubhead stays on the correct path.

It's highly critical to be realistic about what type of swing you need to work the ball around the golf course more effectively. Most country club players fail to admit to themselves that they hit more approach shots from the rough than the fairway. They have nothing to be ashamed of, since even the most accurate drivers on the PGA Tour hit only 75 percent of fairways, while the less accurate drivers hit only about 55 percent. Granted, you'd like to hit a higher percentage of fairways, and I think after applying the swing principles of Nicklaus revealed so far, you will. But it pays to realize that your ball will still land in the rough a few times during a round.

The upright swing will help you hit more greens from the rough and thus enable you to keep low numbers, instead of high numbers, on your scorecard. On par-five holes, the upright plane will allow you to advance the ball farther than you could with a flatter swing, so you can easily make the green in regulation. Therefore, employ an upright swing by incorporating the Nicklaus flying-right-elbow position into your backswing technique.

I said that there was a strong similarity between the backswing actions of Nicklaus, Daly, and Couples. Well, there is also one big difference, which is why Nicklaus wins the accuracy contest. Whereas Couples and Daly let the club swing back past parallel with the clubhead pointing across the target line, Nicklaus swings back into a more controlled position.

In his early days on tour, Nicklaus swung the club back to the three-quarter position. However, once he lost weight and became more flexible, he started swinging the club back to parallel (club-shaft parallel to target line). Either one of these on-plane swing positions will work for you, as long as the club does not arrive in the aforementioned cross-the-line position or in a laid-off position (clubshaft points left of target line). Additionally, you must learn and groove Nicklaus's downswing actions that follow.

THE DOWNSWING

Nicklaus claims he winds his body up so strongly at the top that he feels compelled to start down. Frankly, I think that's an exaggeration. You need to make some kind of move toward the target to initiate the start of the downswing. I do agree that the second half of the swing operates virtually on automatic pilot. I say this because the lapse of time between the top of the swing and impact is so short, again approximately one-fifth of a second. Therefore, the downswing cannot possibly be consciously directed. All the same, there is time to concentrate on one and only one conscious trigger to spark what is essentially an all-out reflexive action.

Once the downswing is triggered, the other movements flow into a sequence and react much like dominoes falling once the first tumbles over. You merely swing *through* positions on the downswing. Yet for you to learn the Nicklaus action, it's important that you be taught the individual elements that make up the second half of his swing. That way, once you're on the driving range, you will be able to develop an action that is one flowing, uninterrupted motion much faster. However, let's first discuss what I think is Nicklaus's most important first movement.

Because Grout was so big on footwork, I believe Nicklaus's first move of the downswing is to simultaneously start replanting his raised left heel and drive his legs laterally toward the target line. It's this dual-action trigger that sets off the domino effect. In two stages, albeit stages that take place in an extremely short time, his knees work back to a square position and his weight moves over to his left side as the foot goes down. Next, his left leg begins to straighten and becomes a solid post for Nicklaus to turn around. Finally, his left hip starts uncoiling.

This entire coordinated movement is very left-side oriented, as it should be if you want to swing well consistently. "Letting the right side dominate this stage of the downswing will almost certainly destroy your golf swing or at least markedly diminish its effectiveness," says top teacher Phil Ritson, who is famous for coaching renowned golf instructor David Leadbetter early in his teaching career. "Any attempt to hit at the ball with your right shoulder, arm, and/or hand will throw the club outside the plane you swung the club back on, and also outside the target line. This damaging over-the-top move also causes the clubhead to come into the impact zone at an undesirable steep angle. The end result of right-side domination for most amateurs is a dreaded slice."

Right-sided dominance is the main reason so many amateur golfers fail to hit good shots even after setting up correctly and making a good backswing. The other reason for their failure is that they try to push or steer the clubhead through impact, rather than using the good turn they've made and freewheeling through the

One reason why Nicklaus is rated as one of the all-time powerfully accurate hitters of a golf ball is that he lets the lower body trigger the downswing action.

ball like Nicklaus. The result is a desperate loss of clubhead speed and poor point of impact. They not only lose distance, they fail to achieve good direction.

Nicklaus never experienced the problem of decelerating the clubhead in the impact zone because Grout encouraged him to hit the ball hard. John Daly, a power hitter in his own right, thinks all golfers should be encouraged to "let the club rip."

Confidence goes hand in hand with aggressiveness. Because Nicklaus built his swing around fundamentals that yielded good results, he played with a strong sense of confidence. You will too. But it is also important for you to manage your power like Nicklaus, who knows full well that the object is to hit drives as far as possible while still being able to keep the ball in the "short grass."

One way Nicklaus promotes solid, well-placed drives is by properly timing the downswing sequence. Replanting his left foot on the ground and vigorously driving the legs toward the target enables him to stretch the left side of his body to the maximum. "This is what obviously gives him the sensation that he is unable to hold back his downswing body release no matter how hard he tries," says teacher Babe Bellagamba of the U.S. Golf Teachers Federation. "Once the downswing is triggered, Nicklaus simply lets go, and allows the sequence to occur. The left hips pulls the midsection, the midsection pulls the shoulders, the shoulders pull the arms, and the arms pull the club."

On the downswing, more and more of Nicklaus's weight shifts to his left foot and leg. Meanwhile, his right hip begins unwinding, his right shoulder lowers, his left hip turns more vigorously around his left-leg post, and the arms pull the club downward into the ideal hitting slot.

What Nicklaus does so wonderfully on the downswing, to max-imize clubhead speed and power, is really work the lower body. "Once the swing has totally changed direction and I put on full throttle, it is always the legs and hips that motivate the club," he wrote in *Golf My Way*.

What Nicklaus failed to tell golfers is that while this thrusting action of the lower body goes on, he keeps his head and upper body back as he waits for the club to swing into impact. Building torque by making the lower body drive toward the target while the upper body tilts back away from the target is not Nicklaus's only power source. He uses a mystery move that top teacher Johnny Myers was the first to identify and share with golfers. As Nicklaus starts down, he slides the front of his left foot inward, so its toe end changes position. It goes from being turned outward to pointing directly at the target line. It's this move that allows his left-leg post to strengthen. This secret action allows Nicklaus to swing at maxi-mum speed with no fear of coming over the top.

Throughout Nicklaus's fabulous career, he has been known for hitting high-flying drives and irons shots that fade, which increase his control and scoring ability, simply because the ball hits its target and stops quickly. Golfers who hit low-flying hook shots have to worry about the ball hitting the fairway or green and run-ning into trouble due to exaggerated overspin being imparted to the ball.

Nicklaus's high-flying ball-flight pattern is a direct result of keeping his head and upper body behind the ball in the hitting area. The lowest point in your swing will always be opposite the center of gravity of your body. When your center of gravity stays behind the position of the golf ball, the lowest point in the swing will also automatically be behind the ball. Therefore, you won't have to make any particular effort to scoop at the ball to hit it solidly, but rather it will happen quite naturally.

"With his upright, modern, power swing, Nicklaus was a very long hitter and he got much of his distance from carry, rather than roll," wrote Ross Goodner in the book *Golf's Greatest*. "This stood him in good stead at golf courses like Augusta National, where his high-trajectory drives and long irons enabled him to carry the crest of the hill on many holes and benefit from a good downhill roll."

As you read these detailed descriptions of the Nicklaus down-swing, I hope you can see how everything works together to produce power. You also can learn to hit the ball powerfully if you practice all of the Nicklaus moves described thus far.

I can't possibly get inside Nicklaus's head, but it's obvious that during his early-day practice sessions he concentrated on delaying the hit by maintaining the hinged position of his wrists until impact. This delayed hit action is just one more of Nicklaus's power secrets. "I call this keeping the club away from the ball as long as possible, and Nicklaus did that really well," says teacher Phil Ritson.

Ritson believes that by delaying the hit, you keep your hands, arms, and right shoulder back, rather than bringing them closer to the ball with that swing-wrecking over-the-top move called the early hit.

While Nicklaus's ultimate goal is to hit the ball with a powerful sweep action, he does not consciously pull the club through. To hit powerfully through the ball, Nicklaus stays down longer than most amateurs, who tend to straighten up in the hitting area. When you do this, the club rises, causing the bottom of the clubhead to hit the top of the ball. If you stay down through impact like Nicklaus, the center or "sweet spot" of the clubface will meet the ball.

Nicklaus's downswing action flows naturally out of the good address and the backswing positions he put himself into previously. Still, to swing through the ideal positions that he learned and practiced and keep the club moving along the correct path and plane, he keeps rotating his left hip counterclockwise. To enhance the thrust of this clearing action, he starts pushing off his right foot, with the heel of the shoe leading the toe end. "As the downswing starts, the strength contained in my right knee is released by pushing off the inside of the right foot," said Nicklaus in the book *My Fifty-five Ways to Lower Your Score*.

As soon as this dynamic push action commences, Nicklaus's left hip recoils at increasingly rapid speed. In turn, his right knee turns inward, and most of his right foot starts lifting off the ground. Additionally, his folded right elbow begins unfolding, and his flexed right wrist begins straightening. More importantly, as Nicklaus drives his right side into his left side, with his head and upper body tilting away from the target, the club is catapulted toward the ball. It really starts whipping faster and faster until it reaches the booming crescendo: impact!

Some of you that are students of the swing might be wondering why I have not mentioned the common instructional word—release. It's certainly not because I want this book to read like an Agatha Christie novel. Frankly, it's because knowing that the downswing happens in a flash, even Nicklaus has no time to think about releasing the club. Besides, the release of the club should happen naturally, not be consciously directed.

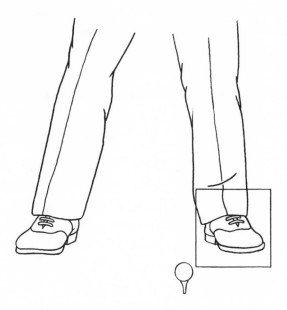

Notice how Nicklaus's left foot position changes, pointing outward when he starts the downswing (left) and pointing directly at the target line at impact (right).

The typical country club golfer has heard the word *release* and has a rough idea that it means to let the right hand rotate back on top of the left in the impact area. The trouble is, the average amateur tries to make this happen early in the downswing by rotating the right forearm over the left and using the right wrist and hand to flick the club into impact. Forget the release, since it happens *after* the hit, not before. More than that, Nicklaus will be the first to admit that it is a result or a response to other techni-

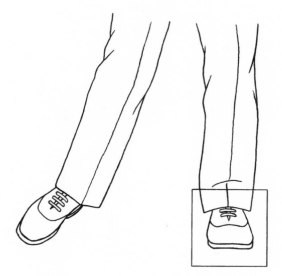

cally correct moves. It is not a move you should think about employing. Because Nicklaus's start-down positions, involving mostly the legs and hips, are so sound, his hands and arms correctly and automatically bring the club squarely and solidly into the ball.

Since impact is the position that matters most, let's take inventory of what Nicklaus looks like when he reaches the moment of truth in the golf swing. Amazingly, the young Nicklaus looks almost identical to Tiger Woods.

Here are my observations of Nicklaus at impact:

Nicklaus's lower body is driving toward the target.

Nicklaus's delayed hit action, shown here, remains one of his most paramount power keys.

Nicklaus's upper body is tilted back away from the target.

Nicklaus's left shoulder is much higher than his right.

Nicklaus's left hip is slightly higher than his right.

Nicklaus's left hip has virtually cleared.

Nicklaus's weight is mostly on his left foot and leg.

Nicklaus's right heel is well ahead of the toe end of his right foot.

Nicklaus's right knee is pointing inward toward the target.

Nicklaus's left arm and clubshaft line up.

If you want a technically sound impact position, copy this one of Nicklaus's. It is one of the all-time best.

The only real difference between Jack and Tiger at impact involves the left wrist. Nicklaus's left wrist is arched or bowed more than Tiger's because he wants the clubface to finish up slightly open and hit a controlled fade. Although Tiger matches the Nicklaus "bowed" position when hitting a fade-stinger shot with a 2-iron, he normally prefers to arrive at impact with his left wrist flat and the clubface slightly closed. The reason is, he prefers to hit the draw or straight shot rather than the fade. If you're wondering why Nicklaus did not ever strive to hit a straight shot, it's because he

In cloning Nicklaus's follow-through position, shown here, make sure that the back of your right hand is parallel to the ball's initial flight line.

believed Hogan when he said, "The straight shot is the hardest shot to hit in golf."

I will take a bet, too, that Tiger's grip pressure is a lot lighter than Nicklaus's, simply because players who prefer to hit a controlled fade grip more firmly with the left hand to prevent the clubface from closing through impact. Players like Tiger who prefer the draw usually grip lightly to more easily swing the club into impact with its face slightly closed.

The follow-through and finish of the swing are simply reactions to the backswing, not conscious actions. Still, you should monitor these positions, looking for very important technical signs that indicate a good (or bad) swing. In the follow-through, the back of your right hand should be parallel to the ball's initial flight line. In Nicklaus's case, this line is slightly left of target, again because he prefers to hit a fade.

When you complete the finish, almost all of your weight should be transferred to the heel of your left foot. Only the toe of your right foot should be touching the ground. As a final check, be sure that your belly button points slightly left of target, or in the direction the fade shot starts its flight. This position proves that you cleared your left side fully and made a free and fluid swing. If you need any further confirmation, look at the ball flying down the fairway.

Special Swing Tips for Seniors

Jack Grout will always be recognized as Jack Nicklaus's true coach. However, over the years Nicklaus has listened to advice from players such as Jack Burke Jr., Deane Beman, and Phil Rodgers, as well as teachers Jim Flick and Rick Smith.

In former days, Flick had watched Grout teach Nicklaus at Frenchman's Creek Golf Club in North Palm Beach, Florida. So he had a good understanding of the fundamentals that the Nicklaus swing was built on. Therefore, it was no surprise that Nicklaus trusted Flick's judgment and asked him to look at his swing during the 1990 Tradition, the first Senior PGA Tour event that Nicklaus played in.

Flick noticed that Nicklaus was exaggerating hip and body action at the start of the downswing, which made it difficult for him

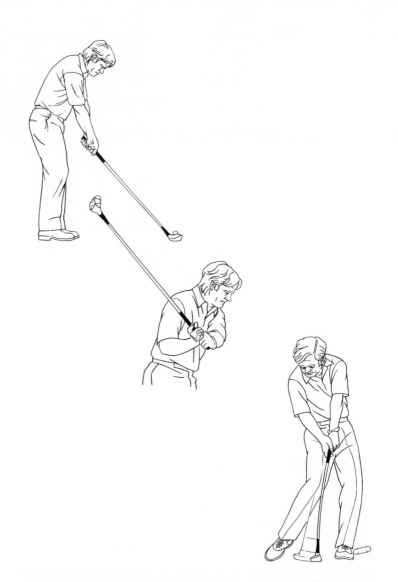

Taking a closed stance (left), swinging down on a flatter shoulder plane (center), as Smith advised Nicklaus to do, and following Flick's active footwork advice (right) will allow you senior players to hit solid shots off the tee and from the fairway grass.

to feel the clubhead and deliver it powerfully into the ball. Nicklaus was hitting weak slices, as a matter of fact. Flick's observations, and his advice to revert back to Grout's instructions to trigger the downswing with the feet, helped Nicklaus regain his form and timing, and win the championship.

Later on in the 1990s, when Nicklaus was reaching an age when he had to make some serious changes to his technique, due mostly to loss of flexibility, agility, and strength, Rick Smith came to the rescue.

Smith told me that, after watching Nicklaus hit hundreds of balls and studying his swing on video, he spotted a major fault. An overly steep downswing plane was hindering Nicklaus's ability to keep the ball in the fairway when hitting drives. Smith had Nicklaus widen his arc, which allowed him to make a deeper turn and swing down from inside to along the target line, rather than outward.

Following Flick's advice to trigger the downswing from the ground up and Smith's advice to widen the swing arc will help you swing the club down into the perfect slot and come into impact with the right shoulder behind your left. Your right shoulder will no longer jut out at the start of the downswing. Therefore, you will no longer swing across the target line and hit a pull slice.

Nicklaus also experiments, from time to time, with a closed stance and a flatter swing in an attempt to hit a controlled draw and gain some distance. If you are a senior golfer who lacks flexibility and feels restricted and downright powerless playing from an open stance, you might also benefit from trying these unique setup and swing techniques. The added bonus of playing this way is that you will pick up some added distance via increased roll due to overspin imparted to the ball. That means you will not need to work so hard to generate such high clubhead speed to hit a power-fade shot.

Nicklaus's Nuances

◆ Nicklaus takes the club back more slowly than any other player, believing that this kind of start helps promote a rhythmic action.

◆ Nicklaus delays the hinging action of his wrists longer than any other player, except maybe Tiger Woods, to help create a wide, powerful arc of swing.

◆ Nicklaus lets his left heel rise higher than any other professional golfer, believing that this allows you to make the freest and fullest possible body coil.

◆ Nicklaus's center of gravity remains on the left side on the backswing, setting him in position to release his arms and club powerfully into the ball.

◆ Nicklaus lets his right elbow fly outward from his body, on the backswing, to ensure an upright plane. Nicklaus believes than an upright swing gives you the best chance of swinging the club along the target line.

◆ As he swings down, Nicklaus's left foot moves from pointing outward to pointing perpendicular to the target line. This foot shuffle helps him—and will help you too—straighten his left-leg post and hit powerfully against his left side through impact.

3 SOLID PREPARATION

*No golfer matches Nicklaus when it comes to
preparing for a championship*

Ever since Jack Nicklaus started playing golf for a living, his chief goal was to win major championships—the four premier tournaments played each year. The Slam is comprised of the Masters, the U.S. Open, the British Open, and the PGA.

The majors are always played on very tough courses, made tougher for each event by narrowing the fairways, making the rough more penal, letting the fringe grass around the greens grow taller, and increasing the speed of the greens by cutting them down to the bone. Very often, too, the course superintendent, under the direction of, say, the Masters Committee members, the U.S. Golf Association, the Royal and Ancient Golf Club of St. Andrews, or the PGA of America, moves the tee markers back much farther or builds new teeing areas to lengthen the course.

Due to the difficulty of major championship courses, players who win on these brutal "tracks" must be able to

1. Hit the ball powerfully off the tee
2. Work the ball left or right, in a controlled manner, both off the tee and onto the green, to deal with dogleg holes and difficult pin placements
3. Hit the ball the proper distance when driving and hitting approach shots, to land the ball on a level area of fairway grass and leave the most level putt possible
4. Play controlled wood and iron shots into a headwind and know how to take something off the shot when hitting downwind shots
5. Recover from the rough intelligently and proficiently, either hitting a safe shot back to the fairway or cutting the ball out of the grass and hitting it onto the green
6. Hit pitch shots that stop quickly on the green, run up to the hole, or spin back toward the hole
7. Chip the ball close to the hole out of heavy grass surrounding the green, using a good degree of imagination and "soft hands" to manipulate the clubface into an open impact position and hit a quick-stopping shot
8. Hit high, soft sand shots that carry the high bunker lip, "check" upon landing on the green, then trickle toward the hole
9. Possess exceptional feel in the fingers, employing the right size and speed of stroke to putt the ball the proper distance
10. Exhibit steadiness of nerve to employ a solid arms-and-shoulders-controlled stroke and sink short pressure putts

In addition to being a skillful swinger and tee-to-green shot-

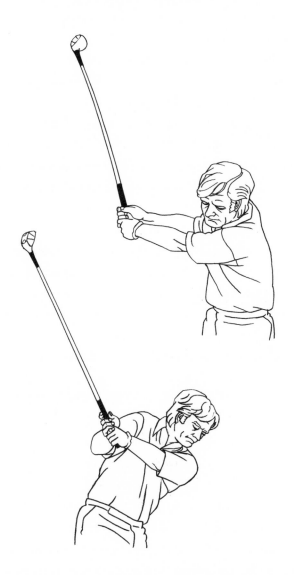

One chief reason why Nicklaus—once golf's terminator—could win on any
course was that he had mastered the upright swing plane (top), necessary for
hitting a left-to-right fade shot, and the flat swing plane (bottom), necessary
for hitting a draw shot that flies gently from right to left.

maker, the golfer who wins a major must also be a smart planner before and during the four days of a championship.

During the decades of the 1960s, 1970s, and 1980s, when Nicklaus was really on top of his game, he arrived at a championship venue early and started studying the course as intently as a boxer who watches films of an opponent prior to a championship bout. Nicklaus realized the more he knew about a particular course, his true opponent, the better his chances of making the right offensive and defensive moves, minimizing mistakes, shooting low scores, and winning.

Typically, with his caddy close to his side, Nicklaus arrived at a major championship venue almost two weeks prior to the start of the event. His reasoning, according to what he said on the Golf Channel, was he wanted time to work on his game and feel so comfortable with his swing and the course that by the time the tournaments started he knew how to handle it. "Other players who arrived just before the tournament often didn't feel comfortable with the course until the third round, when it was too late," said Nicklaus.

During practice rounds, Nicklaus familiarized himself with the course, making adjustments along the way, particularly if holes had been lengthened, a new bunker had been added, a new type of sand had been added to the bunkers, and greens had been reconstructed or featured a new type of grass.

Changes in the course design usually meant that Nicklaus would need to change his equipment or alter it, and sometimes even switch to a different shot-making strategy. For example, if the sand was exceptionally firm due to dryness or wind, Nicklaus would consider using a sand wedge with less than ten degrees of bounce.

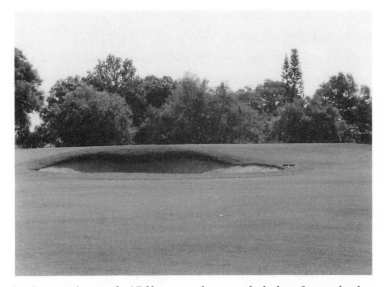

During practice rounds, Nicklaus was always on the lookout for new bunkers or bunkers with new sand, and he took the time to familiarize himself with them. When playing a practice round on an "updated" course where you are to compete, keep your eyes open for changes in design that will cause you to alter your strategy.

Bounce means the degree to which the back or rear edge of the club's flange lies below the leading edge of the flange. The purpose of bounce is to allow the flange to slide through the sand like a knife through butter. Without this bounce feature, the leading edge of the clubhead would dig into the sand behind the ball.

Nicklaus still plays with a sand wedge with a medium flange, but he has been known to change to a bunker club with a bigger flange if he encounters "soupy" sand during his practice-round preparation. Additionally, he makes sure that his pretournament preparation schedule includes practicing hitting out of firm sand with a pitching wedge that features a sharper leading edge and thus allows him to knife the ball out.

Nicklaus has always been so creative in his preparation for a big tournament that he once put a one-ounce plug of lead under the grip of his driver before the U.S. Open, to promote better feel, slow down his hand speed, and thus allow him to hit more fairways. Prior to playing in the 1967 U.S. Open at Baltusrol, which Nicklaus won, he switched to a Bull's Eye putter purposely painted white to block out any distracting glare from the bright New Jersey summer sun. This putter, nicknamed "White Fang," was also

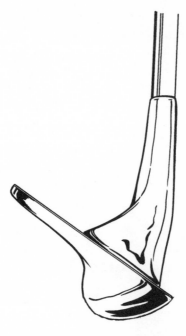

The bulge at the base of the sand wedge, referred to as "bounce," makes it easy for the club to slide through the sand and lift the ball out.

lighter, which helped Nicklaus pace the ball to the hole more consistently on the course's superfast putting surfaces.

There's no question that Nicklaus should be rated golf's ultimate mastermind, and this claim is further supported by the way he still maps out a course prior to a Senior PGA Tour major championship, recording important features in a little memo pad he carries in his pants pocket. It's obvious that this diligent preparation works, considering that Nicklaus has three PGA Seniors' major championship wins to his credit: the 1991 U.S. Open, in which he defeated Chi Chi Rodriguez in a play-off, the 1991 PGA, and the 1993 U.S. Open.

During practice rounds, Nicklaus walks the course, mapping out each hole. On his memo pad, he uses circled areas to designate the best areas to land a tee shot, darkened areas to designate dangerous hazards to the side of the fairways or greens, and tiny Xs to represent the course's subtle and treacherous slopes in the greens. He also marks off any changes to the course, such as a newly expanded green or bunker, with an asterisk. He does this, knowing from experience that a new strategy is likely in the cards. For example, if a new long bunker is added to the left side of a fairway, he might need to hit a draw on that particular hole. If a tee on a par-three hole is extended or a green extended to bring into play new pin placements, he knows he would have to consider changing the way he normally plays the hole.

Nicklaus also uses the practice-round time to test out different clubs. On a narrow par-four hole, for example, he alternates between hitting a 3-wood and a long iron to see which club, under calm and windy conditions, allows him to land the ball in the best spot in the fairway for an attacking approach shot.

If you swing too fast, do what Nicklaus once did: put lead tape under the grip on your driver to increase the swing weight of the club so that you slow down your swing.

Nicklaus no longer arrives at a major championship as early as he used to, due usually to a heavy course-design schedule or family responsibilities. However, in the old days he practiced playing a tournament course for at least a week. Consequently, when the time came to play the actual four-day championship, he was prepared for anything.

When competing for a championship title, Nicklaus knew what club was best to hit off a particular tee if the wind was at his back. He

When playing a practice round on a redesigned course, look for collection areas like this one to the side of the green. Then, when playing the same course in a tournament, avoid these at all costs by fading the ball onto the green whenever possible, just as Nicklaus did so often during major championships.

was sure that a particular iron would land his ball close to the hole on an approach shot into a strong wind. He knew how to handle a hole if the fairways and greens were wet or extra dry. Furthermore, Nicklaus knew what subtle changes had to be made to his setup and swing, should weather conditions change. Here's a case in point: When the wind howled during a British Open, he felt comfortable moving the ball back in his stance on approaches onto the green and hitting a knockdown shot, simply because he had already worked on this on a windy practice day prior to the start of the championship.

"When it came to judging wind direction, the heaviness of air, the speed of the fairways and greens—even the effects of dew—Jack

Nicklaus and Ben Hogan were the best," said Tiger's former coach, Butch Harmon. "As good a player as you are, you'll never reach the next level of becoming a scratch player if you don't take the time and care to weigh all conditions. If you want to shoot par scores, simply give yourself time to think strategic thoughts."

Nicklaus's exceptionally diligent practice gave him another advantage over players who arrived at a major only a couple of days before it commenced: a stronger sense of confidence. Golf reporters were correct in saying Nicklaus sometimes seemed cocky. Well, they said the same thing about Arnold Palmer, Cassius Clay, Babe Ruth, Mario Andretti, and John McEnroe. And now they say it about Tiger Woods. The fact is, confidence is built from hard work and determination, whereas cockiness is often a result of non-preparation and insecurity.

I touched earlier on equipment and how Nicklaus sometimes replaced one club for another after determining during a practice round that a particular driver, sand wedge, or putter worked better. Now I'd like to bring up the subject of equipment again, and relate it to Nicklaus's game and yours.

Throughout his career, Nicklaus tinkered with clubs, which is understandable when you consider that he played McGregor clubs and eventually was involved with working on club designs. But Nicklaus did not just try a new club out. He made sure that every club in his bag fit him perfectly, as you should too. Only if the shaft flex, lie, loft, length, grip size, and weight of your clubs are suited to you will you be able to make the best possible swing and play the golf you are capable of playing. Nicklaus went to great lengths to be custom fitted, realizing that playing with the right clubs for you is part of the preparation process.

The statement, "A good golfer can play with any club," is only partially true. Unless a club matches your body shape, hand position, height, natural strength, and swing tendencies, you will fail to live up to your full potential as a player. Nicklaus knows this, as do other top-notch players who would rather play with an old club that fits them than a new club that does not.

Golfers who play with noncustom clubs, no matter how popular the brand name, are cheating themselves because they will never develop into consistent players. The reason is, if a club is not fitted to your build, strength, setup, and swing tendencies, your subconscious mind will make compensations in your swing and cause you to develop bad habits. A properly fitted club will allow you to set up comfortably, swing correctly, and hit good shots. Therefore, let me review some of the more important elements of a golf club that Nicklaus paid the most attention to when playing his best golf and still does today.

SHAFT FLEX. Whether your clubs feature graphite or steel shafts, shots you hit right of target and extra low signal a flex that's too stiff. Balls that fly left of target and extra high indicate that the shaft is too flexible for your strength and swing speed.

Nicklaus is strong and generates high clubhead speed, so he needs a stiff shaft to ensure that he returns the club squarely and solidly into the ball at impact. To hit shots that start flying at the target on a relatively flat trajectory, then rise quickly into the air, maybe a medium-flex shaft is for you. My advice is to experiment like Nicklaus did, testing out "demo" sets of clubs, available in your local country club pro shop or custom club shop, until you find a shaft flex that works for you.

LIE. Lie is simply the angle the shaft makes with the ground when the club rests on the grass. Tall players usually require an upright-angle club, while short players need a flat-angle club. The chief consideration in choosing a club with the correct lie is how high or low you set your hands at address. Once a player sets up to the ball, the bottom of the clubhead must be virtually flush to the ground. Actually, if a dollar bill can just be slipped under the toe end of the clubhead, the lie is correct. If the toe sticks up considerably, the club is too upright. If the heel is off the ground, the club is too flat to suit the player's hand position.

Jack Nicklaus feels more comfortable at address and confident about playing good shots when he sets his hands rather high and close to his body, much like Tiger Woods. Nicklaus, standing five-eleven, needs clubs featuring a lie angle that's two degrees more upright than standard. This lie-angle feature of the golf club should not be taken lightly. If the lie of the club is incorrect, as even Nicklaus discovered, you will experience swing and shot-making problems. That's because you will be forced to change your swing path and plane to suit the angle of the club and thus employ a very unnatural feeling technique.

While working in England, I learned from former British Open champion Henry Cotton something even many club-makers do not know. Hitting a lot of practice shots can actually change the lie of your iron clubs. Nicklaus obviously knows this, because part of his pretournament preparation involves having the lie angle of his iron clubs checked for inconsistencies.

LOFT. Loft is the degree of pitch built into the clubface. Depending on the degree of loft, the ball will fly high or low.

Nicklaus uses a much less lofted driver than he did in years gone by. That's because back when he was winning majors in the 1960s and 1970s, metal clubs were not available. Nicklaus played with clubs made from persimmon wood. Today's metal drivers and fairway clubs are much more sole-weighted, so they lift the ball into the air more easily. Consequently, a high degree of loft no longer has to be built into the clubface.

Nicklaus's irons are kicked back in slightly too now, meaning that the modern-day 7-iron, for example, is equal to the old 6-iron in the degree of loft built into the clubface.

Whether you play with newer clubs or older models really does not matter. What matters is this: if your shots fly extra low, you should be fitted with more lofted clubs, and if you hit extra-high shots, you should be fitted with less lofted clubs.

LENGTH. A player's height has little to do with being fitted for length. The distance of the player's hands from the ground is the most critical factor when being fitted. Players with short arms usually need longer clubs, while players with long arms should swing shorter ones.

Nicklaus is an exception to the rule. He has short arms, but because he likes a club to sit on an exaggerated upright angle, he can get away with using a driver that is much shorter than standard. Ironically, Tiger Woods also plays with a driver that's shorter than standard length.

As a rule, longer clubs, particularly drivers, allow you to swing the club on a wider arc and hit the ball longer, while shorter clubs allow you to hit the ball more accurately. Nicklaus also swings a shorter-length club because he considers control his priority. Sure, he could hit the ball much longer by using a longer driver, but the ball would probably land in the rough more often too, owing to his need to make swing compensations.

When making your choice, remember that the player who hits the ball in the fairway the most times is usually the player who shoots the lowest score. You must appreciate, however, that it will do you little good to hit a weak but accurate drive in the fairway. So find a length of club that allows you to hit the ball solidly but accurately too.

GRIP SIZE. Next to shaft flex, proper grip size is the most important feature of a golf club. If the grip is too thick, it prevents the player from feeling the clubhead and stops the player's wrists from working fluidly. The tendency is to deliver the club into the ball late with the clubface wide open. The result: a slice. Grips that are too thin encourage loose hand action and ultimately cause the clubface to be closed at impact. The result: a hook.

Generally, to promote feel and better control of the clubhead throughout the swing, a player with a small glove size should be fitted with thinner grips. Golfers with a large glove size will do better with handles that are built up slightly. Players with standard-size hands should stick to a stock grip.

The two most common type grips are rubber and leather. Most golf professionals and low-handicap amateurs prefer rubber. Nicklaus likes the feel of leather grips. Nicklaus also favors slightly oversize grips, mainly because they prevent him from overworking his hands and wrists in the impact zone and allow him to hit his classic fade shot.

WEIGHT. An extra-light club tends to cause a player to swing very fast and lose control of the club. A heavy club tends to cause the player to lose vital clubhead speed and deliver the club into the ball with the face open. Nicklaus still prefers a slightly heavier club because he is strong, but as the years go by, he's destined to switch to a much lighter club.

In your case, choose a club that's light enough to allow you to generate ample clubhead speed, say eighty miles per hour, and heavy enough for you to feel the clubhead.

NICKLAUS'S SECRET MENTOR: THE FAMOUS GOLFER WHO TAUGHT NICKLAUS ABOUT PREPARATION

When I conducted my research for this book and discovered how intelligent Jack Nicklaus was about equipment, and about preparation in general, I immediately thought of Ben Hogan, since he had constantly tinkered and experimented with his clubs, even going so far as to insert a longer driver shaft into his 3-wood so he could swing on a wider arc and hit the ball longer.

I also found it interesting that Nicklaus had inserted lead tape under his grip for added feel, and to thicken the grip so that he was less apt to overwork his hands and hit a hook. Hogan, by coincidence, it seemed, had added extra wrappings of tape under his grips, too, also to prevent a hook and promote fade shots. I might add that Hogan was more eccentric than Nicklaus. He did such things as drink ginger ale before a big tournament because he learned from a concert pianist that the ginger in the ale takes the puffiness out of the fingers. As a result, Hogan's feel for the club was enhanced, making it easier for him to hit the ball the proper distance. Who knows? Maybe there was something to Nicklaus constantly eating those oysters when he first came on tour.

When I reminded myself that Nicklaus, like Hogan, also wrote down information about the course during practice rounds, then referred to his notes during play, I started to think this was more than a coincidence. However, I figured this could not be possible, particularly because to my knowledge Nicklaus had never mentioned any association with Hogan. Besides, Hogan rarely talked to anyone. Puzzled, I decided to inquire, going first to Greg Hood, a former personal assistant of Hogan's.

According to Hood, he had heard that Hogan and Nicklaus played together several times, but he did not know where and when. Also, during a discussion with Hogan about Nicklaus, Hogan told Hood that Nicklaus used to watch him practice and asked him questions, namely what he thought about during practice rounds, the eve of a championship, and while he was hitting balls.

I heard about Hogan being a stern, grouchy guy, and how after his 1949 car collision he became supercold and solitary, so the story sounded false. In the back of my mind, though, I remembered some other Hogan anecdotes that Hood had shared with me when I was doing research for a book I was writing, *The Hogan Way*. Back then, all of Hood's stories about Hogan checked out. Still, I had my doubts for several reasons:

1. Nicklaus never mentioned any such stories about Hogan in what he called his magnum opus, the book *Golf My Way*.

2. I had been in the golf writing business for twenty-five years, including working for *Golf Illustrated* magazine in England from 1980 to 1982, and *GOLF Magazine* from late 1982 to 1998, and never heard any stories about a Hogan-Nicklaus association.

3. I have attended umpteen press conferences and never once heard Nicklaus mention Hogan's name.

4. I was in attendance at *GOLF Magazine*'s 1988 Bicenten-
nial Dinner honoring Player of the Century Jack Nicklaus, along with golf's other living heroes, including
Hogan, who was present, and never once heard Nicklaus
mention his name.

5. I had spoken to Nicklaus three times in my life about
golf, and he never mentioned Hogan.

In a further conversation with Hood, I really pressed him, but
he could remember no more than he told me. So I knew, journalis-
tically, that I had to continue seeking out other sources that could
confirm what Hood had told me and, if possible, be more specific.

I spoke to several fellow writers and magazine editors, but drew
a blank. Next, I checked with a number of golf memorabilia deal-
ers, but came up with nothing. Then one day in an antique shop,
among old books, I found a copy of a book I had never heard of:
The Greatest Game of All, circa 1964, by none other than Jack
Nicklaus.

In this book, Nicklaus talks nostalgically about playing with
Hogan during the 1960 U.S. Open at Cherry Hills Country Club
in Denver, Colorado; during practice rounds for the 1961 U.S.
Open at Oakland Hills Country Club in Birmingham, Michigan;
and over a long stretch of years during practice rounds for the Masters played every April, at Georgia's famed Augusta National Golf
Club. But that wasn't all. On page 28, Nicklaus says this: "I have
had the pleasure of playing quite a number of rounds with Ben
Hogan. I always learn something from watching Hogan."

Once I had this confirmation, I started making comparisons and
discovered similarities in how these two golfing greats prepared for
major championships.

The way Nicklaus scopes out the course during practice rounds, noting in a pad what clubs he hit off certain tees and onto greens in certain conditions, as well as designating what greens are particularly slow or fast or what sand bunkers feature firm or soft sand, is very reminiscent of Hogan's preparation process.

After a practice round, Nicklaus, like Hogan before him, returns to the practice range to work out any kinks in his swing. Hogan was actually the first player to start the postround practice trend. Nicklaus followed in his footsteps, learning that the only way to feel confident going into a championship is to fix a fault in your swing.

On the eve of a championship, Nicklaus mentally plays the course in his mind, shot by shot. Hogan took this preparation to the extreme by mapping out his strategy on a blackboard before retiring to his hotel bed. Still, it's obvious that Nicklaus learned the value of mental preparation from Hogan.

Prior to teeing off, Nicklaus, like Hogan, keeps to himself, taking time to gather his thoughts in the locker room and walking slowly to help induce a relaxed state of mind. Hogan did the same things; however, he did go the extra mile, driving his car extra slowly to the course to trigger a trancelike state of concentration.

Nicklaus's preround practice sessions, like Hogan's, were all business, and included mental and physical rehearsals of the shots that were likely to be played on the course.

Whatever the shot Nicklaus is likely to play in a major championship he's about to compete in—power fade, draw shot, high ball, low ball, extra-high long iron, soft pitch, lob wedge, long sand shot, lag putt, or short pressure putt—he rehearses it mentally first, seeing the perfect shot come to life in his mind's eye. Next, he methodically sets up, aiming at a specific target as if he were hitting a shot that counted during competition. Again, Hogan took things to the extreme when rehearsing a curving shot. When practicing a draw or fade, he would go to the end of the range and try to wind the ball around a real tee, instead of being satisfied with imagining one.

Like Hogan, Nicklaus only concentrates on one swing trigger when practicing shots. However, again like Hogan, he would use a different swing thought for a different shot. For example, in hitting a drive he might think, "Slow back," to encourage a smooth take-away, and when hitting a running chip, "Let the hands lead the clubhead into impact." Like Hogan, too, if he hits a bad shot, say on a practice drive, he will try a different swing thought or a different physical action and keep "reloading" until he gets it right. That's because, like Hogan, Nicklaus believes that the harder you practice, the better you get.

Good golf, as you see, is a result of hard work. No matter how good you are at present, in order to stay good or learn to play better and shoot lower scores, you must take the time to

1. Get to know your course and how to play it in varying conditions.

2. Mentally rehearse the shots you will need to play the evening before an important competition, say the club championship.

3. Give yourself plenty of time to get to the course before a match, to induce relaxation and preserve your energy and focus by doing everything just a little bit more slowly than normal.

4. Practice hitting shots that you will need to play during the round, and I don't just mean drives.

If Nicklaus knew he was likely to hit short delicate pitch shots out of high fringe grass, he'd prepare by practicing opening the clubface at address (left) and hitting the shot until he had figured out what trajectory was best (right).

5. Allow some time to practice chips and putts, so you can see how the ball reacts in the air and on the ground with different clubs. That way, you will be prepared to chip the ball close to the hole, lag a long putt up close, or knock a pressure putt in.

Good preparation also means sometimes spending time away from the course or practice tee—getting away from it all. Fishing, skiing, tennis, and hunting allow Nicklaus to relax away from the

course. His ability to escape is why he is still able to play competitive golf and still enjoy the game. You will enjoy golf more, too, if in preparing for a big club match or championship, you make time for other outlets involving sports, hobbies, or family activities.

Nicklaus's Nuances

♦ During his heyday, Nicklaus arrived at a major championship up to two weeks early, to study the course and figure out his shot-making strategies. Learn the course you are to compete on well too. In fact, map out each hole, as Nicklaus has always done.

♦ Nicklaus experiments with different golf clubs, usually sand wedges and putters, to see which one works best on a particular course. Follow his example, and you will cut strokes off your score.

♦ Nicklaus is a very creative player, always looking for ways to improve his shot-making skills and score. He once put lead tape under the grip of his driver to promote added feel and played with a putter painted white to block out distracting glare from the sun. Use you imagination, too, and you might stumble on something that works wonders.

♦ Part of Nicklaus's pretournament preparation includes carefully checking the features of his clubs, such as the lie. You, too, will benefit from making sure your clubs are in good order before an important game.

◆ Nicklaus was fortunate to play many rounds with
   Ben Hogan, who taught him to do such things as
   concentrate as hard in practice as in play. Seek out
   low-handicap players and ask for advice to help you
   bring your game to the next level.

SHOT-MAKING MADE SIMPLE

*Learn how to minimize setup and swing
changes when hitting creative shots—the Jack
Nicklaus way*

Even in the past, when Nicklaus won or came
close to winning almost every tournament he
entered, he was never accused of being an
exciting player to watch. Nicklaus did not, and does
not, exhibit the swashbuckling style of Walter Hagen, Arnold Palmer, Seve Ballesteros, or even Tiger
Woods, who is known for really letting it all hang out
on the course and playing superaggressively.

Nicklaus's shot-making reputation was built around
control. Still, Nicklaus, like every other golfer, did
and still does make the occasional error and lose the
firm hold on his consistent game when his swing is
not quite right. In such cases, especially when playing a very demanding golf course, he has to make creative recovery shots. Still, he goes about his business
methodically and depends on simple setup and
swing keys to bail out. In short, Nicklaus is not the
most exciting player to watch, but he has always been
the most methodical. What's ironic is that Nicklaus

admits to learning how to play some creative shots from some very exciting pros, most notably Chi Chi Rodriguez.

Since I have worked at home and abroad writing for golf magazines, I have had the rare opportunity to travel to many tournaments and watch Nicklaus in action. Winning shots are always great, but when they are hit in the heat of a major championship, they mean something more. A player's true talent shows up. Only if his technique is solid will he be able to hit great shots and finish the job. Nicklaus knew how to do that better than anyone, particularly during the Masters, U.S. Open, British Open, and PGA championships. Let's not forget, too, the shots he hit en route to winning two Senior Open championships and one Senior PGA.

I will never forget the time Nicklaus removed his sweater on the final hole during the 1970 British Open at St. Andrews before proceeding to drive the green; or the time he hit a 1-iron stiff to the hole on the par-three seventeenth hole during the final round of the 1972 U.S. Open at Pebble Beach; or his back-nine heroics at Augusta National, during the final round of the 1986 Masters. His performance in the play-off for the 1991 U.S. Senior Open at Oakland Hills, when he shot 65 to beat Chi Chi Rodriguez, was something else too.

I bring up just these few instances to remind you how great Jack Nicklaus was, which for some is hard to remember after watching Tiger Woods play. As good as Tiger is, he has a long way to go to match Nicklaus. Besides, when Nicklaus played through the decades of the 1960s, 1970s, and 1980s, there were more great players to challenge him, most notably Arnold Palmer, Gary Player, Seve Ballesteros, Greg Norman, Lee Trevino, and Tom Watson. Most of the time, Nicklaus withstood their challenges because of his ability to follow a simple system of hitting shots that enabled him to handle pressure situations.

To illustrate the simplicity of Nicklaus's shot-making methods, I now will take a few pages out of the history books and analyze when, where, and how he played a variety of winning tee-to-green shots. What I think you will notice right away is how Nicklaus's setup and swing keys—the same ones he uses today—are far less complex than those taught today by many teachers around the country.

THE CONTROLLED DRAW-DRIVE

When and Where Nicklaus Played This Shot

Nicklaus's most famous major championship victory came at the 1986 Masters, when at the age of forty-six he beat all the young "flat-bellies" and other golfing legends and foreign champions. Moreover, he shut up a couple of newspapermen who before the tournament had written him off, claiming it was time for the Golden Bear to retire.

Going into the last round, Nicklaus was behind, but thanks to a birdie at the tenth hole and an eagle at number thirteen, he shot a 6 under par of 30 on the back nine to edge out veterans Tom Kite and Greg Norman by a single shot and win his sixth Masters. On the holes mentioned, Nicklaus gambled and perfectly executed power-draw drives, turning the ball around the corner to effectively shorten the hole and make it easier for him to play aggressive approach shots.

Although Nicklaus's bread-and-butter shot is still a fade, knowing how to hit a draw helped him win several major championships, including the 1986 Masters.

How to Copy Nicklaus's Shot-making Method

Align your feet and body right of target, on the line you want the ball to starts its flight. The bigger the draw you want to hit, the farther right you should aim. Point the clubface at the area of the fairway where you want the ball to land.

Swing normally, then just watch as the ball flies nicely along a controlled right-to-left draw-path.

The 3-Wood Drive

When and Where Nicklaus Played This Shot

Not once, but several times, Nicklaus chose to play this shot off the tee during the 1966 British Open championship played over the famed Muirfield Links in Gullane, Scotland. This shot also helped him shoot a 17 under par score of 271 in the 1991 PGA Seniors' championship, played at PGA National Golf Club in Palm Beach Gardens, Florida.

Because of this intelligent strategy, Nicklaus kept the ball in play and put himself in ideal positions for scoring birdies on his way to victory.

How to Copy Nicklaus's Shot-making Method

Tee the ball up lower than normal, make a strong coiling action in the backswing, replant your left foot at the start of the downswing, and strive for a high finish to promote good arms-club acceleration through impact.

Towering Long-Iron Tee-Shot

When and Where Nicklaus Played This Shot

In 1972 Nicklaus hit one of the all-time great shots on the par-three seventeenth hole at Pebble Beach Golf Links, during the U.S. Open. It was a soaring 1-iron that hit the flagstick, stopping just a foot from the hole. A tap-in birdie helped Nicklaus chalk up a third win in this coveted championship.

Most golf experts still consider Nicklaus the greatest long-iron tee-shot player ever. He certainly proved how great he was during the 1972 U.S. Open at Pebble Beach.

How to Copy Nicklaus's Shot-making Method

This is considered anything but a standard shot, so don't play the ball off the left heel, Nicklaus's standard position. Instead, position the ball opposite your left instep.

On the backswing, concentrate on making a strong body coil and let the right elbow fly, Nicklaus style. Coming down, concentrate on keeping your head behind the ball through impact.

Three-Wood Fairway Shot

When and Where Nicklaus Played This Shot
This shot came in handy en route to Nicklaus's 1975 PGA win at
Firestone Country Club in Akron, Ohio, particularly on the long
par-five sixteenth, where he was able to overpower the hole.

How to Copy Nicklaus's Shot-Making Method
In playing this shot off lush fairway grass, like at Firestone,
set up and swing as you would to play the classic Nicklaus
power-fade tee shot, but play the ball back slightly behind the
left heel.

Tailoring the Tip: In playing off tight fairways, like those at Baltusrol, where Nicklaus first won the U.S. Open in 1967, hinge your
wrists quite early in the take-away to help promote a steep arc of
swing and descending blow. Additionally, slide your legs more vigorously toward the target through impact to help you hit the ball
with a slightly open clubface and fade the shot.

Running Long-Iron Fairway Shot

When and Where Nicklaus Played This Shot
A "hot" 3-iron shot that Nicklaus hit to the fourteenth hole during
the last round of the 1966 Masters was a chief reason he won the
championship. Nicklaus had driven the ball into the trees on the
420-yard par four, leaving him a much longer second shot than
normal. Knowing that the green would not hold even a superhigh

As Nicklaus proved in the 1966 Masters, he's also a master of playing low, long-iron fairway shots. When playing such a shot, follow Nicklaus's example of striving for a more rounded finish position like the one shown here.

shot, he decided to hit the ball low so that it would land short of the green and run up to the hole.

Everything went better than Nicklaus planned. The ball ran up and came to rest three feet from the hole. A birdie putt allowed him to start a comeback run and win.

How to Copy Nicklaus's Shot-making Method

The four most important keys to making this shot are playing the ball back slightly in your stance, making a more rounded backswing turn, exaggerating arm rotation in the through swing, and striving for a more rounded follow-through.

CUT MEDIUM-IRON SHOT

When and Where Nicklaus Played This Shot

The sixteenth hole at Augusta National, a par three called Bluebell, looks innocent, yet it remains one of the most treacherous in all of golf. Nicklaus will admit that if you get greedy and attack the flag too aggressively on Sunday, you could end up overshooting the green and scoring double bogey.

In the 1963 Masters, Nicklaus was tied for the lead coming to this hole. Because the hole was positioned back right, definitely in a "sucker pin" position, Nicklaus decided to start the ball left of target and cut the shot in, so the ball would fade toward the hole and land extra softly. The ball did just that and more. It stopped some four yards short of the hole. Nicklaus proceeded to hole the birdie putt and go on to win, once again due to smart shot-making.

How to Copy Nicklaus's Shot-making Method

Select one more club than is needed for the distance, for example a 5-iron instead of a 6-iron, and open the clubface slightly. Make sure you take either a neutral or even a slightly weak grip. Play the ball off your left heel and stand closer to the ball with your hands set higher than normal.

Swing the club back outside the target line, then swing up to the three-quarter position and stop. Swing down slightly across the ball, holding on more firmly with your left hand to hold the clubface open.

UPHILL IRON SHOT

When and Where Nicklaus Played This Shot

During the opening round of the 1963 Masters, heavy winds caused the ball to roll down hills and up others. Nicklaus did a great job of playing from lies he had never before confronted during practice rounds. In fact, he did such of good job of hitting these shots that he won the championship. His same shot-making prowess off uphill lies helped him win the 1991 PGA Seniors' championship at Michigan's Oakland Hills Country Club.

How to Copy Nicklaus's Shot-making Method

Play the ball closer to your highest foot. Set up perpendicular to the slope and give yourself essentially a flat lie by tilting your body away from the target. Hitting off an uphill slope will cause you to increase the effective loft of the club at impact, so compensate by taking one more club than normal for the designated distance.

Make a slightly shorter swing than normal and concentrate on swinging your arms rather than on making a huge body turn. Don't worry about generating enough power to propel the ball to the green. Remember, you solved this problem by taking one more club.

DOWNHILL IRON SHOT

When and Where Nicklaus Played This Shot

During both the 1970 and 1978 British Open championships that Nicklaus won at St. Andrews, he had to play this shot a few times.

As expected, each time he played a supercontrolled on-target shot, which is the reason he twice held the famed claret-jug trophy high above his head.

How to Copy Nicklaus's Shot-making Method

Play the ball closer to your higher foot and set your body at a right angle to the slope. Keep adjusting yourself until you feel confidently comfortable about your address.

Take one less club (i.e., a 7-iron instead of a 6-iron) to allow for the effective loft of the club decreasing at impact. When the club comes into impact this way, the shot flies lower and the ball runs farther.

Make a normal backswing, but when swinging down, "chase" the ball down the slope and keep your left knee flexed through impact to prevent a pull.

BALL-ABOVE-FEET SHOT

When and Where Nicklaus Played This Shot

Nicklaus ran into this lie more than once during the 1980 PGA at the Oak Hill Country Club in Rochester, New York.

Fortunately, his youthful experience playing at Scioto Country Club in Columbus, Ohio, helped him recover. At Oak Hill, Nicklaus played these shots brilliantly with short and medium irons and went on to win the championship.

How to Copy Nicklaus's Shot-Making Method

In setting up, align your body square to the target. Choke down on the club slightly. Open the clubface to counteract the natural right-to-left spin that will inevitably be imparted to the ball. The more severe the slope, the more you should open the clubface.

Swing normally, but a little bit more slowly, so you maintain good balance and hit the ball cleanly.

BALL-BELOW-FEET SHOT

When and Where Nicklaus Played This Shot
Regardless of how good a strategist Nicklaus is, he still did not manage to avoid having to play this shot en route to winning the 1980 U.S. Open at Baltusrol, one of the world's hilliest courses. However, because he remembered what Grout taught him to do during his youth, he was able to easily handle this lie.

How to Copy Nicklaus's Shot-making Method
Set up with your weight more on the heels to help you retain balance. Close the clubface more or less, depending on how severely the land falls away from you.

Make a normal backswing.

On the downswing, be sure to keep your knees flexed and eyes focused on the ball as you pull the club into impact.

RIGHT-TO-LEFT CROSSWIND SHOT

When and Where Nicklaus Played This Shot
In the 1970 British Open at St. Andrews, Nicklaus played this shot well under pressure, both during regulation play and during his play-off with Doug Sanders, who finished second.

How to Copy Nicklaus's Shot-making Method

In this wind condition, do what Nicklaus usually does: play a fade shot, so that the ball hits the wall of wind blowing from the right and drops down softly to the green.

At address, play the ball midway between your feet in a slightly open stance, and open the clubface slightly. In swinging back to the three-quarter position, concentrate on extending your arms and club away from the ball and keeping your wrist action minimal.

In swinging down, drive your legs laterally so you feel the club lagging behind your hands. Keep your left hand bowed outward through impact.

Left-to-Right Crosswind Shot

When and Where Nicklaus Played This Shot

In the 1978 British Open, Nicklaus hit the ball left of target and let the wind bring it back toward the hole. I guess he did this because he feared hitting a boring right-to-left shot that pitched on the green and ran through it. Like Nicklaus, let the left-to-right wind do the work for you.

How to Copy Nicklaus's Shot-Making Method

Aim your body and the club left of target. Obviously, the stronger the wind, the more you should aim left. Take one more club if the wind is severe.

Make a compact, controlled backswing and swing through to an imaginary target left of the real one.

The ball will fly into the air and work its way back to the hole.

Stop Shot From a Fairway Bunker

When and Where Nicklaus Played This Shot

This is not a shot Nicklaus played often during his prime, because he rarely strayed from the fairway. Nevertheless, he did have to play this shot during several major championships, most notably during the 1962 U.S. Open at Oakmont, a course in Pennsylvania known for its numerous bunkers. The main reason he had no trouble hitting the ball cleanly is because he is known as a "picker" rather than a "digger" when it comes to shot-making style. In other words, he sweeps the ball rather than go down after it.

How to Copy Nicklaus's Shot-making Method

The higher the lip, the more lofted the club you should select. Play the ball just short of the midpoint in an open stance, with about 70 percent of your weight on your left foot.

Swing normally. The address position will promote a sharp, clean hit.

Light Rough Iron Shot Recovery

When and Where Nicklaus Played This Shot

The pressure was on Nicklaus when he came to the final hole of the 1963 Masters, played at the very demanding Augusta National Golf Club in Augusta, Georgia. But there was even more pressure building in his brain and body after he pulled his drive into the left rough. The reason Nicklaus felt the heat was that he knew he had to hit the green, and keep the ball on it, then two-putt for par. He did all that he needed to do, beating Tony Lema by a single stroke.

To hit high, soft-landing iron shots from light rough, like the one Nicklaus played en route to winning the 1963 Masters, keep your head behind the ball through impact.

How to Copy Nicklaus's Shot-making Method

Take one more club than normal, relative to the number of yards to the green, and open the clubface slightly. Play the ball forward in an open stance with your hands slightly behind. Place slightly more weight on your right foot.

Make an upright, compact backswing.

Swing down, keeping your head behind the ball to help you make contact on the upswing. These two keys will allow you to hit a high shot with a little bit of cut-spin so that the ball flies high and lands softly.

Deep Rough Recovery

When and Where Nicklaus Played This Shot

Nicklaus's shot-making talent and strength when hitting recovery shots from deep rough helped him win the 1966 British Open championship, played at Muirfield.

How to Copy Nicklaus's Shot-making Method

Take one less club to offset the flyer effect that occurs when grass intervenes between the ball and clubface at impact. Close the clubface too, to compensate for the club opening at impact due to the thick grass. Play the ball well back in your stance so you are set up to hit down into the ball as sharply as possible.

On the backswing, hinge the right wrist early so you promote a very steep plane.

On the downswing, lead the club down into the ball with your left hand and hit down hard with your right.

Knockdown Iron Shot

When and Where Nicklaus Played This Shot

Nicklaus pulled his drive into the left rough on the seventy-first hole during the 1986 Masters. Forced to hit a low shot, he hit the ball to eleven feet, sunk the birdie putt, and went on to win.

How to Copy Nicklaus's Shot-making Method

Play the ball just behind the midpoint in a square stance with your hands positioned a couple of inches ahead of it.

One of Nicklaus's major swing keys for playing the knockdown shot is letting the hands lead the club into impact.

Make a normal, compact backswing.

On the downswing, shift your weight to your left foot as soon as possible and let the hands lead the clubface into the ball.

BITING SHORT IRON

When and Where Nicklaus Played This Shot
One of the better short-iron shots Nicklaus ever hit came at the short, but often treacherous, seventeenth hole in the final round of the 1965 Masters.

The pin was on the right side of the green, but toward the back. Nicklaus's caddie, Willie, wanted him to hit a pitching wedge, especially since he knew that if Nicklaus hit the ball over the green, it would land in deep trouble. Nicklaus chose a 9-iron, but hit it with such stopping power or "bite" that it came to rest a foot from the hole. Nicklaus scored an easy birdie and went on to win his second straight green jacket, given to winners of this prestigious championship.

How to Copy Nicklaus's Shot-making Method

Position the ball just behind the midway point in a narrow stance, so that your hands are a couple of inches ahead of it. Put 60 percent of your body weight on your left foot.

Swing the club back on the same upright plane established by the upright lie of the short iron, but let your wrists hinge very freely.

Swing the club down into the back of the ball, keeping the follow-through action short. To help you use a hit-and-hold action, pretend you are hitting into an old tire. Henry Cotton, the two-time British Open champion, used to do this in practice.

ONE-BOUNCE AND SUCK-BACK SHOT

When and Where Nicklaus Played This Shot

In the 1963 PGA championship, contested at the Dallas Athletic Club in Dallas, Texas, Nicklaus faced a short-iron third shot on the par-four eighteenth hole after hitting a poor tee shot into the rough and chipping back out to the fairway. He hit a 9-iron shot twenty feet past the pin, which bounced once before "sucking back" close to the hole. This shot set up a relatively easy par that helped him secure victory.

Whenever you face a short-iron shot to a front pin, and the green's guarded by trouble, don't risk hitting into it by trying to play a finesse shot. Instead, hit a one-bounce and suck-back shot.

How to Copy Nicklaus's Shot-making Method

Play the ball a few inches behind your left heel, so that 70 percent of your body weight is on your left foot, and the clubshaft is tilted toward the target.

Make a short backswing, controlling the action with your arms and not your hands.

Tilting the shaft toward the target is one secret to playing the one-bounce and suck-back shot—Nicklaus style!

In swinging down into the ball, concentrate on accelerating your arms and chasing the ball with the club. That way, you will take a long, thin divot and keep the clubface on the ball a split second longer, increasing the spin effect.

HIGH, SOFT-LANDING PITCH SHOT

When and Where Nicklaus Played This Shot
En route to winning the 1965 Masters, Nicklaus shot a record score of 64 in the third round. One memorable shot that helped set him up for a fourth-round cakewalk, and a nine-stroke victory over

Nicklaus's compact swinging action helps him hit controlled short pitch shots "stiff" to the hole.

Arnold Palmer and Gary Player, was a high-lofted pitching wedge that he hit to two feet from the cup on the seventh hole.

How to Copy Nicklaus's Shot-making Method
Play the ball off your left instep and set up open to give yourself a strong sense of bodily freedom.

Keep the backswing short for pitches up to sixty yards and let the wrists hinge freely. On longer pitches, lengthen the swing, or else you'll tend to feel the need to quicken your swing tempo.

On the downswing, rotate your right hand under your left to help you scoop the ball up high off the grass.

PITCH-AND-RUN

When and Where Nicklaus Played This Shot
This shot helped Nicklaus win all three of his British Open championships—in 1966, 1970, and 1978. The reason: whereas American courses feature hazards guarding the front of the greens, the links courses of the British Isles feature clear entranceways that allow the golfer to run the ball up to the hole.

Many modern-day American courses are being modeled after links courses, so you had better learn how to play this shot, particularly if the pin is located on the green's top tier, the surface is firm, and the wind is at your back.

How to Copy Nicklaus's Shot-making Method
Play the ball inside your left instep in a square or slightly open stance. Experiment to see which stance feels most comfortable and yields the best results.

Employ a half-swing that is slightly flatter than normal.

On the downswing, rotate your right forearm over your left, so the toe of the club leads the heel and you impart a small degree of draw-spin on the ball. Draw-spin causes the ball to roll slightly faster to the hole, so you can maintain your normal tempo even when hitting to an uphill pin placement.

LONG BUNKER SHOT

When and Where Nicklaus Played This Shot
This shot made it possible for Nicklaus to beat Isao Aoki in the 1980 U.S. Open, played at New Jersey's Baltusrol Golf Club.

How to Copy Nicklaus's Shot-making Method
Set up virtually square to the target, open the clubface only slightly, and widen your stance a little.

On the backswing, turn your shoulders clockwise to promote the desired shallow backswing arc and stop when you reach the parallel position.

On the downswing, really accelerate your arms and the club. Use your right hand to slap the sand behind the ball and cut out a very shallow divot.

Tailoring the Tip: When the ball is buried, use a pitching wedge, square the clubface at address, swing on a steep plane, and hit down sharply to knife the ball out.

One chief technical "must" for playing a long bunker shot is taking a thinner cut of sand.

SHORT BUNKER SHOT TO TIGHT PIN

When and Where Nicklaus Played This Shot

Thanks to playing a few expert short bunker shots, Nicklaus was able to win both the 1962 U.S. Open at Oakmont County Club and the 1971 PGA at PGA National in Palm Beach Gardens, Florida.

How to Copy Nicklaus's Shot-making Method

Go through a preswing checklist, making sure to set up open, choke down on the handle of the sand wedge, position the ball off your left instep, and lay the clubface wide open so it points at your final target. Also, before swinging, imagine cutting out an area of sand that starts two inches behind the ball and stops six inches ahead of the ball. One more thing you must do at address is to wriggle your feet down into the sand. For some strange reason, many senior players I've observed fail to do this. Don't make the same mistake, because digging your feet down into the sand will help you build a firm foundation for employing a balanced swing.

Swing the club back to the halfway point on a fairly upright plane.

Turning the right hand under the left through impact enables Nicklaus to keep the clubface open and hit a high, soft-landing bunker shot.

On the downswing, concentrate on slapping the sand with the bounce of the club and turning your right hand under your left hand to keep the clubface open. This technique will allow you to blast the ball up high, so that it carries the lip of the bunker and lands softly on the green.

THE LOFTED CHIP

When and Where Nicklaus Played This Shot

Nicklaus still recalls the fifty-foot wedge chip he hit into the cup for birdie at the third hole during the 1962 U.S. Open. It was this chip that boosted his confidence and relaxed him over the tough Oakmont course, where it's easy to face a chip and walk off with bogey or worse. His frame of mind was so good, he went on to beat Arnold Palmer and begin the Nicklaus era of golf.

How to Copy Nicklaus's Shot-making Method

Play a sand wedge and open the clubface slightly at address. Take a narrow, open stance with the ball played forward in your stance. Place about 60 percent of your weight on your left foot. Stand closer to the ball than normal, with your hands behind it slightly. Keep your left arm (guide arm) more rigid than your right arm (power arm).

On the backswing, leave the majority of your weight on your left foot, keep your head perfectly still, and hinge your right wrist quite dramatically as you swing the club straight back. Keep the entire backswing action compact and swing rather lazily or slowly.

In swinging down, let your right wrist and right hand release under your left hand and left wrist. The ball will pop up into the air, land near the hole, and roll slowly toward it.

A forward ball position is critical to hitting a lofted chip shot.

THE RUNNING CHIP

When and Where Nicklaus Played This Shot

During the 1973 PGA championship at Canterbury Golf Club in Cleveland, Ohio, and the 1975 Masters at Augusta National in Augusta, Georgia, Nicklaus hit several running chips close enough to the hole on par fours to save par easily and score birdie on par fives.

How to Copy Nicklaus's Shot-making Method

If your favorite chipping club is an 8-iron, take a 9-iron for this shot.

Play the ball back in your stance so your hands are positioned well ahead of it. Literally, give yourself some extra elbow room by standing a little farther away from the ball than you would if playing a lofted chip.

On the backswing, swing the club slightly inside the target line, using only enough wrist action to promote good feel for the club-head.

On the downswing, rotate your forearms counterclockwise to close the club's face slightly at impact and impart a slight degree of hook-spin on the ball.

Setting your hands well ahead of the ball is critical to hitting a running chip shot.

LONG CURLING PUTT

When and Where Nicklaus Played This Shot

In a final round dogfight with Tom Weiskopf, at the 1975 Masters, Nicklaus took command of the tournament when he holed a forty-five-foot left-to-right breaking putt on the sixteenth green. This putt secured victory, especially after Weiskopf scored bogey on the same hole. Thanks to holing this "snake," Nicklaus won an unprecedented fifth Masters title.

You are not likely to compete for the Masters, but you very likely will face a long curling putt at your home course. Therefore, learn and groove Nicklaus's technique.

How to Copy Nicklaus's Shot-making Method

Imagine the ball curving and rolling toward the hole before you start your stroke, since this mental exercise will help you feel the right pace.

Take a slightly wider stance than normal to encourage a longer, low-back and low-through stroke. Be sure, too, to hold the club more lightly in your hands so it can swing like a pendulum, but firmly enough to allow you to easily control the path of the stroke.

Let the big muscles in your arms control both the back and through stroke, accelerate the putter through the impact zone, and don't look up until the ball is struck. If you find you have trouble getting your pace right and tend to come up short consistently, let your right wrist hinge slightly on the backswing to enhance feel, then just let it straighten on the downswing.

Nicklaus is still an exceptionally good long-range putter because he swings the putter like a pendulum.

SHORT PRESSURE PUTT

When and Where Nicklaus Played This Shot

Nicklaus won the 1962 U.S. Open at Oakmont Country Club in a play-off against Arnold Palmer. But had it not been for holing out a four-foot pressure putt on the seventy-first hole of regulation play, Nicklaus would have lost by a shot to Palmer. He hit the ball firmly into the center of the cup. This putt was so significant to his career that he admits, "I get goose pimples just thinking of that short putt."

Nicklaus made another significant career move in the 1993 U.S. Senior Open, played at Colorado's Cherry Hills Country Club, when he holed several short putts during the final round to beat Tom Weiskopf by a single stroke.

Whether you are playing a Nassau match at your country club, competing in a tournament, or trying to break you own record score, sooner or later you will need to hole one of these "knee-knockers." Copying Nicklaus's technique is thus a smart strategy.

I bet if golf pros, sportswriters, sportscasters, and country club golfers were polled, all but a few would choose Nicklaus to hole a short pressure putt if their life depended on it.

How to Copy Nicklaus's Shot-making Method

Set up comfortably, with the ball opposite your left instep or toe, and your eyes directly over the target line. This address will allow you to see the line more clearly and encourage you to swing the clubface through the ball and directly at the hole.

It's best to control the stroke with the bigger muscles of your arms, since the slightest degree of hand action can throw the putter off track. Keep the putter moving low on the way back and on the way through, since this will help you roll the ball more smoothly across the putting surface.

Nicklaus's Nuances

◆ Nicklaus's shot-making skills were enhanced by watching great players, such as Ben Hogan and Jack Burke Jr. Always look to better players or experienced pros for innovative tips, and never be afraid to experiment hitting different shots with different clubs.

◆ Nicklaus relies more on mechanics than he does on feel. You also will benefit from developing a simple and systematic set of swing principles that are related to the shot you are called upon to hit during a round of golf.

◆ Nicklaus's simple formula for playing the power-fade shot is to aim the feet and body left of target, point the clubface at the final target, and swing normally. Follow his example.

◆ One chief reason why Nicklaus turns so fully and hits such strong, high, soft-landing long-iron shots is because he lets his right elbow fly on the backswing. Allow yourself the same freedom, no matter what anyone tells you.

◆ Nicklaus's upright plane helps him hit out of the rough. Therefore, you would be smart to swing on a more upright than flat plane.

◆ In hitting sand shots, Nicklaus focuses more on taking out an area of sand, rather than hitting a specific spot behind the ball. You will find it easier to hit good bunker shots if you apply the same technique.

◆ When playing a running chip, Nicklaus swings the club through the ball from open to closed. This path causes the clubface to close slightly at impact, so that overspin is imparted to the ball. In turn, the "hot" running ball runs nicely to the hole. If you have a problem hitting chips short of the hole, try Nicklaus's unorthodox but proven method.

◆ Nicklaus lets his right wrist hinge slightly on long

putts. To promote added feel for distance, copy his technique.

◆ Nicklaus is a die putter rather than a charge putter. If you hit long putts well by the hole, and end up three-putting, change over to the Jack Nicklaus way of putting.

5 MASTERMIND

The reasons why Nicklaus is rated golf's all-time best on-course thinker and strategist

At the nineteenth hole, following a round of golf, the conversation among amateur golfers often turns to the question of whether golf is mostly a mental or a physical game.

In answering this question, developing a solid set of fundamentals relative to setting up and swinging is of paramount importance. Having said that, once you learn to employ an effective technique and can hit a variety of basic tee-to-green shots as well as more creative ones, such as the controlled fade that Jack Nicklaus made famous, golf is played entirely between the ears.

"Great players such as Jack Nicklaus and Tiger Woods thrive on the pressure situation that causes lesser golfers to falter, precisely because the mental side of their game has been that much stronger than their competitors," famed golf coach Butch Harmon told me when we collaborated on the book *The Four Cornerstones of Winning Golf.* "I believe that average golfers can do as much to improve the mental side of the game (and with it, their course management skills) as they can in any area of the mechanics of the game."

Golf is a game that can never be perfected, namely because of the swing's complexities. In addition, because we are human, our bodies cannot be expected to work as efficiently as a machine and repeat the same exact swing motion over and over. Some days we feel strong and physically flexible, and on other days we feel weak and stiff. Consequently, no golfer ever masters the swing to such a degree that every shot over eighteen holes is perfect. Even Nicklaus admits to being stronger in some areas of the game than in others. For example, as he has said often in press conferences, he is a better long-iron player than driver of the ball, and a much better putter than short-iron player.

Well, you are probably asking yourself, how did he win so many championships? The answer, my fellow golfers, involves the *mental game*. Nicklaus's mental mastery is what has allowed him, throughout his long ongoing career, to

1. Prepare intelligently for a championship
2. Plan out a shot strategically
3. Pick the proper club
4. Picture the perfect shot
5. Play the highest-percentage shot that best allows him to hit the ball from point A to point B
6. Persist for the entire round
7. Preserve strokes by not playing stupid shots
8. Play patiently
9. Put himself in front in a tournament and stay there
10. Play confidently enough to dominate golf for three decades

Nicklaus believes what sports psychologist Glen Albaugh believes: "You can create a sense of confidence by merely thinking positively, even when you are not on top of your game."

If you never had the opportunity to watch Nicklaus when he was the guy to beat on tour, you missed something special. From the second he stepped onto the first tee to the time he stroked his last putt into the hole, he looked superconfident and gave every shot 100 percent concentration. In fact, he once commented that he never missed a shot in his mind before he actually swung the club. He still plays this way mentally.

Nicklaus remains the all-time tactical master of the golf course, who never plays a shot he's not sure he is capable of hitting. That's not to say every shot comes off as planned. It's to say that because of clear and realistic thinking, he gives himself every opportunity to hit the best possible shot.

To Nicklaus, a good drive is not measured according to how far you hit the ball. The shot you hit off the tee, more than anything else, must be hit in a strategic area of the fairway that allows you to attack the hole on your approach shot. For example, a drive hit 250 yards to a level area of the fairway on a 350-yard par-four hole is better than a 300-yard drive that leaves you playing your second shot from a steep downhill slope.

Nicklaus's criteria for measuring a good approach shot is not always related to how close you hit the ball to the hole. For example, when playing in the Masters at Augusta National, he considers a shot ten feet below the hole on a sloping green better than a shot hit five feet above the hole. On superfast undulated greens, you can charge most uphill putts with no fear of three-putting. That same philosophy will not work when putting downhill on slippery putting surfaces. In fact, sometimes when the pro golfer is so fearful of knocking his first putt well by the hole and three-putting, he gently coaxes the ball to the hole.

During a round of golf, you'll inevitably run into sundry situations, some more mind-boggling than others. Your playing capabilities on the day, common sense, confidence, and a constant battle with your ego will all be factors when you decide on the line you want to hit the ball along. The secret is realizing that you are the master of you own destiny. Know what you can and cannot do with a particular club, and don't take unnecessary risks.

Many amateurs stay high handicappers because they allow their ego to run the show. Because of the machismo factor, they often hit far less club than is required and almost always attack the flag. Don't make the same mistakes, or you will waste strokes. Unless you are in the ideal position in the fairway to go at the flag, play for the center of the green, as Hogan taught Nicklaus to do.

While playing with Hogan, Nicklaus obviously learned the value of sensible strategic planning and taking the safer route when playing shots. Of course, there were times when Nicklaus gambled. But when he did, he always felt the percentages were in his favor, which is a smart philosophy to adopt.

When hitting a more aggressive shot, Nicklaus is also prepared for the consequences. For example, he attacks a back-tier pin to set up birdie if and only if he knows that if he overshoots the hole, the fringe grass or bunker is not so severe that he may have a difficult time saving par.

"If Jack is in contention, particularly in a major, he becomes so conservative in his club selection that, if he mishits the ball, the damage will be minimized," says Jim Flick, who Nicklaus considers one the world's best teachers. "Other times, he can be so bold it seems foolhardy—until you see the results."

As former Masters and British Open champion Sandy Lyle once told me, "The game of golf is a lot like chess. The only difference being that your true opponent is not your fellow competitor but the course itself. Therefore, rather than having checkmate as your goal, you should concentrate on hitting fairways and greens and keeping double bogeys off your scorecard."

Planning golf intelligently involves a lot of variables, including knowing exactly how far you hit each club. Sure, in order to gather this information you must sacrifice playing golf with friends and spend time alone on the practice range, hitting shots and noting how far you carry the ball on average with every club in your bag. If you want to become a true strategist and really lower your handicap, you'll spend a couple of hours each week hitting short-game shots too, such as a lofted chip, and then mentally and physically keep a record of how far the ball carried and how far it rolled.

Nicklaus trained hard under teacher Jack Grout, listening to every word of advice from this experienced instructor. He also spent hours and hours practicing the movements of the swing and keys to shot-making, all the time as determined as Mozart was to improve as quickly as possible and expand his horizons. He practiced until he grooved a swing he could depend on, realizing it would never be flawless.

Even today, when Nicklaus's swinging action fails to operate at maximum efficiency and he starts hitting an uncharacteristically shaped shot, he is smart enough to play for that "new" type of shot and still shoot a decent score. Other less intelligent players try to fix their fault midway in the round and end up shooting high scores and missing the cut. Not Nicklaus. The only time he plays the Mr. Fix It role is after the round, when he hit balls until he figures out the root cause of his wayward shots.

A cautious and logical playing strategy is another of Nicklaus's strong points. When standing on the tee ready to tee off, he studies such conditions as wind, the contour and firmness of the fairway, the severity of the rough, and the position of the pin before selecting a club out of his bag.

"As my game improved, I became more and more intrigued by the way in which the elements that make up the golf course determine the type and quality of shots a golfer is called upon to play," wrote Nicklaus in a 1974 *Sports Illustrated* article. "Seeking to understand each new hole I encountered, I tried to put myself in the head of the course architect. Inevitably, this intense observation improved my strategic approach to shot-making, which led to better scoring, which encouraged me to develop an ultra-analytical approach as a competitive tool."

Nicklaus is particularly savvy on par-three holes, knowing that they present the golfer with less margin for error because the target green is smaller than a wide expanse of the fairway.

If Nicklaus selects a driver on a par-four or par-five hole, he usually hits a power fade. This left-to-right shot is a much more controlled shot than the hook because even if it flies off line, it stops quickly once it lands. A hook, on the other hand, rolls with overspin, often into the rough or trees.

Should you choose to play a fade over the draw, be sure to follow Nicklaus's intelligent setup procedure: tee the ball closer to the right tee marker, then aim down the left side of the hole to give your shot room to take shape. If you tee up on the left side of the tee box, par-

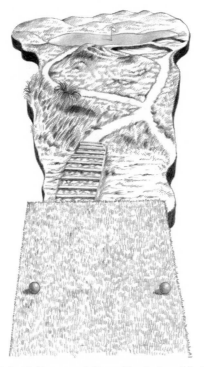

Before selecting a club, Nicklaus carefully studies the lay of the land of a partic-ular hole and figures out the strength and direction of any wind. You should too.

ticularly on a narrow, tree-lined hole, the ball will probably hit the trees before it has a chance to curve back toward the fairway.

On approach shots, Nicklaus again usually plays the fade, namely to avoid hazards and because the ball sits down quickly on fast greens. Oh, what a pleasure it is to watch Nicklaus. He seems to hit the ball into the stratosphere. Then the high-hit ball floats down like a parachute and sits softly on the green, "like a hound dog in front of a fireplace," to borrow a line coined by CBS golf commentator Jim Nantz.

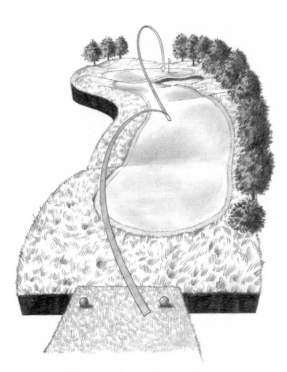

Whenever possible, Nicklaus prefers to play a fade shot, both off the tee and on approach shots.

Whether Nicklaus hits the characteristic fade or a draw onto the green, selecting a specific target is always in his master plan. He focuses on a section of the green up ahead to help satisfy his mind as to the type of shot he wants to hit. Selecting the proper target must be based on such conditions as the lie of the ball and the contour and firmness of the green, wind direction, and the tempo and rhythm of your swing on the day of play. If the lie is good, you might want to consider gambling and attack the hole. However, should a sense of uncertainty creep into your head, be smart and widen your target to include the fat of the green, particularly when playing a long-iron shot into a firm green, with the pin cut close to the back of the green.

"What separates Nicklaus from players such as Lee Trevino, who talked a lot in between shots, is his all-business attitude on the course," says Tiger Woods's former coach, John Anselmo. "When Nicklaus walks off the tee and down the fairway toward his ball, he already starts thinking hard about working out a shot strategy in his mind. What's more, when he does shoot a high score on a hole, he leaves the green, then walks to the next tee unbothered, putting past performances behind him as if letting a door close."

Regarding club selection, Nicklaus uses the "fifteenth club"—his brain—to figure out which "stick" will allow him to hit the ball in the best position. Moreover, he never lets his ego get in the way by trying to be Superman, stretching a club beyond its limitations

When Nicklaus finishes a hole, it's as if a door closes behind him. He never brings mental baggage to the next tee.

by swinging fast. Learn a lesson here. When puzzled between playing, say, a hard 8-iron instead of a smooth 7, select the stronger club to avoid pressing and mishitting the ball. As Nicklaus has proved throughout his great career, this strategy is virtually foolproof. Because courses are designed with water hazards in front of the greens and bunkers to the side, even if you hit the ball over the green with a less lofted club (in this case, the 7-iron), you'll face a fairly easy pitch or chip shot and still be able to salvage par.

Nicklaus is probably the smartest approach player ever. If the pin is on the right side of the green behind a bunker, he usually hits a shot well left of the hole and lets the ball drift toward it. If the pin is tucked left, he sometimes hits a soft draw over the right bunker and lets the ball curve toward the hole. In playing a shot to an elevated green, he knows from experience that you have to hit one more club than normal because it plays longer than the yardage. When hitting to a green well below him, such as on the seventh hole at the Pebble Beach Golf Links in California, he usually takes one club less (i.e., a pitching wedge instead of a 9-iron). He follows this strategy knowing that effectively the hole plays shorter than the yardage on the card, due to the considerable drop in elevation from tee to green.

Nicklaus is able to hold his score together when hitting into trouble, too, again because he plays with his head, not his heart. If he lands in deep rough, for example, he does not compound the error by getting angry, then trying to pull off the impossible shot. Sensibly, he swallows his pride and plays a short shot back to the fairway. Nicklaus is so conscious about not wanting to wreck a good score that even when facing a short shot out of a buried lie in a high-lipped bunker, he has been known to sometimes aim for the fat of

Nicklaus has always been able to swallow his pride when hitting into trouble. Instead of gambling and compounding a problem, he is so mentally disciplined that he sensibly plays a shot back to the fairway.

the green, even if that means shooting away from the pin. His logic: I can still save par by rolling in a long putt, or at worse score bogey.

Nicklaus is equally intelligent on the greens, adopting strategies that prevent him from cornering himself into a three-putt situation. First and foremost, he takes great care to read the break in the green, so that he can determine where the ball is going to start curving. Second, according to veteran teacher Gary Wiren, who reported on the special thoughts of Jack Nicklaus in the classic book *PGA Manual,* "The long time Nicklaus spends crouching over the ball ready to stroke is not to focus on to mechanics but to wait for the right feeling that the putt is going in." Third, unlike Tom Watson, who was famous for charging the cup, Nicklaus is a die putter. Most times the ball seems to barely make it to the edge of the cup, then drops slowly into it. Only when hitting putts of fifteen feet or less does he charge the hole.

When you analyze Nicklaus's game, it's amazing how simple and basic his playing philosophy is. Realizing that a good start to a round lifts your confidence, he concentrates extra hard on the first tee. I have to think it was Ben Hogan who talked to Nicklaus during one of

Nicklaus never plays a breaking putt before he carefully "reads" the slopes in the green.

their practice rounds together and emphasized this point over and over. I say this because Hogan once described his first-tee mental strategy, as follows, in an interview with Nick Seitz of *Golf Digest* magazine: "I would take longer on the first tee than I would any other place on the golf course. I was gearing my brain. Taking a look at the fairway. Taking three or four practice swings. A lot of people wondered what I was doing up there. Why I didn't tee the ball up and hit it. I was organizing myself to play the round. I thought harder about that first shot than any shot I played. It set the tone for the day."

Once he gets a good first hole under his belt, Nicklaus stays calm and collected over each shot, taking time to gather his thoughts and put himself in an emotional comfort zone. Nicklaus focuses hard on the course but never gets overexcited by the importance of the moment, which sports psychologist Bob Rotella thinks is highly critical to achieving peak performance. Furthermore, Nicklaus never lets himself get distracted, which is a quality also reminiscent of Hogan.

"Nicklaus pays as much attention to the sounds around him as he would a passing wind," says renowned sportswriter Bert Randolph Sugar. "His concentration is so intense that he divorces himself from everything around him, and concentrates on the only thing that matters: his golf game."

Nicklaus does not try to overpower the golf course into submission either, even though he is still quite powerful off the tee. Based on mistakes made early in his career, he realizes how concentrating on power rather than precision leads to off-line shots and high scores. His priority: positioning the ball off the tee and hitting greens in regulation.

Nicklaus's strategy is in sharp contrast to that of the weekend player, who often plays with a new driver that promises extra yardage off the tee and follows a go-for-broke strategic philosophy. Oh, sure, there are some golfers who swing hard just so they can tell their friends in the clubhouse how far they hit the ball off the tee on a particular hole, and only had a wedge left onto the green. However, these are usually the same golfers who post high scores due to hitting other long and wrong drives they don't ever tell anybody about.

Nicklaus, like Hogan, is also very aware of some finer points involved in teeing off that make all the difference when trying to post a low score. For example, he stands behind the tee markers, looking first at his target. Next, he looks at the actual teeing area and picks out a level spot to tee up his ball and compensate if the tee markers aim toward the woods rather than the center of the fairway.

On par-three holes, Nicklaus is sly like a fox, too. In watching him play these one-shot holes at various championship venues, I noticed some strategic nuances that involve the way he tees up the ball and prove he's always concentrating on ways to out-think the course.

Nicklaus tees the ball about a half inch high when playing long irons and just above the grass or about one-quarter inch high when setting up to play a short iron.

In preparing to hit a low shot, he tips the tee slightly forward. When setting up to hit a high, soft shot downwind or to a tight pin placement, he tips the tee back slightly. These tee-up nuances may seem like small potatoes, but they are actually unrevealed secrets that will help you hit better shots and shoot better scores.

On par-four and par-five holes that curve left or right, or "dog-

leg," as golfers say, Nicklaus tees the ball up lower to help promote
a more upright swing and fade shot, and higher when playing a
draw.

When hitting approach shots, Nicklaus normally hits the ball on
a high trajectory, particularly when attacking a hole that's on a firm,
fast green. However, he is a smart strategist who knows the advantage of playing a low shot into wind, as he did on so many links
courses when formerly competing in the British Open.

Speaking of playing into a strong wind, rather than trying to
swing out of his shoes on an approach shot on a very long par-four
hole, and risking landing in trouble, he smartly lays up short of the
green, where he can play a wedge for his third shot from the fairway
and still save par.

In hitting approach shots, especially third shots on long,
unreachable par-five holes, Nicklaus takes the time to pace off how
many yards the ball is from the pin, or waits for his caddy to give
him the exact yardage to the front, middle, and back of the green
before playing the shot. It is this intelligent planning process that
allows him and will allow you to select the right club, swing at the
proper speed, and hit the ball close to the hole.

When choosing a club, take another page out of Nicklaus's
golden rules of strategy book. Pick the club that will allow you to
reach the green without hitting it superhard. Nicklaus employs a
powerful swing, yet he always swings smoothly and stays balanced.

Nicklaus also depended on his imagination when playing golf,
as you should. When playing an iron shot out of a fairway bunker,
imagine the sand as grass. This preswing imagery will eliminate
anxiety and body tension and increase your chances of picking the
ball cleanly off the sand just like Nicklaus. When hitting a wedge

over water, focus your eyes on top of the pin, instead of at the hole. This mental focusing will take your mind off the water hazard and encourage you to make a slightly fuller swing and hit the ball all the way to the hole. I still love to watch Nicklaus hit wedge shots over the top of the flag and spin the ball back to the hole.

Nicklaus uses his head when playing shots around the green, too. In hitting chip shots, for example, he does not always reach for a favorite club. He uses his imagination and plays out different shot-making scenarios in his mind to help him pick the right club and shot. He calls this process "going to the movies."

When playing long putts on fast greens, he sees the ball just reaching the cup, then plopping into the hole, since this helps him pace the ball gently across the green.

In hitting short uphill putts, I was told that he imagines a second hole a few feet past the real one to encourage a firm, confident stroke. When hitting a short downhill putt, he imagines a second hole a few feet in front of the actual one. This strategy will help you ease the ball to the hole.

Nicklaus, guided by his teacher Jack Grout and other mentors, had to learn the value of playing smart golf slowly but surely. He now knows that smart golf means sometimes hitting a fairway wood or long-iron off the tee on a very narrow hole or one that curves sharply left or right. Intelligent golf also means aiming for the middle of the green instead of the hole when the risk outweighs the reward, and lagging a putt up close to the hole rather than charging it and risking knocking the ball well by and three-putting.

If you are serious about lowering your handicap, you must think the same way. You must also be prepared to spend some quality time alone after the game, analyzing your round. That's the only way you can pinpoint strategic error patterns and correct them. Nicklaus did that throughout his entire career, and what a job he has done.

Although Tiger Woods is turning the golf world upside down, I agree with ABC golf commentator Peter Alliss: "Nicklaus's record of dominance is unparalleled."

Nicklaus's Nuances

◆ With regard to the mental side of the game, Nicklaus is a true 10 on a 1 to 10 scale, and that is one of the chief reasons he has won so many golf tournaments around the world. Make mental-game improvement one of your goals, and you will see your scores drop.

◆ Nicklaus is all business on the course. Once standing on the first tee, he goes into a mental cocoon of intense concentration and never lets up until sinking his final putt. You, too, should try as hard as you can to stay focused for all eighteen holes.

◆ Nicklaus's strong mind allows him to remain patient in the heat of battle and not press when he's behind in a championship. You will also benefit from keeping cool and not trying to force a good score by taking silly risks.

◆ Nicklaus is so mentally disciplined that he does not get upset after hitting a bad shot. If you make a bad swing, hit a bad shot, or score badly on a hole, put the experience behind you.

◆ Nicklaus is intelligent enough to know that on the golf course, precision is more important than power. When playing, concentrate on hitting fairways and greens, not on trying to hit 300-yard drives.

◆ Nicklaus depends on his imagination on the golf course, by letting several shot-making scenarios play out in his mind. This same strategy will help you select the right club and hit the right shot.

◆ Nicklaus never hits a putt until he sees it fall into the hole in his mind's eye. This positive mindset will enhance your confidence and encourage you to make a pure putting stroke.

Afterword

Jack William Nicklaus is now purely a Senior PGA Tour player. He rarely competes on the PGA Tour or in the four major championships that make up the Grand Slam: the Masters, U.S. Open, British Open, and PGA. Yet, with a record eighteen majors to his credit, and shrines devoted to him at golf's Hall of Fame in Florida, at Golf House, the U.S. Golf Association's home in New Jersey, and at the new museum built on the campus of Ohio State University to honor its former student and golf star, we are constantly reminded that Jack Nicklaus is the all-time greatest golfer.

Nicklaus has also won three Senior PGA Tour major championships—two U.S. Open championships and a PGA—and he just might surprise us once again. Any one who doubts this possibility need only remind themselves of Nicklaus's historic victory in the Masters, at age forty-six.

There is no give-up in Jack Nicklaus. There never has, and there never will be. As a junior player, he rose above the competition. As an amateur, he won two U.S. Amateur titles. As a PGA pro, he was the man to beat every week. And as a senior player, he has done more than hold his own. In fact, in the fall of 2002 he teamed with Tiger Woods to beat legendary player Lee Trevino and young superstar Sergio Garcia.

Beyond Nicklaus's playing career, there is his course-design business to keep him competitive. He continues to build some of the best courses in the world, with Muirfield in Dublin, Ohio, rated as his number-one masterpiece.

The Nicklaus name will forever be synonymous with excellence. He knew how to play the course better than anyone, and off the course he is still at the top of his game when it comes to being a golf ambassador.

Nicklaus did things the old-fashioned way: he earned everything through hard work and dedication, and that is precisely why the new superstar in the world of golf, Tiger Woods, has chosen him as his model.

Nicklaus has been a model of mine, too, and I am honored to have made a connection to this immortal champion through *The Nicklaus Way*. I'm confident that, once you absorb and apply the instructional material just presented to you, you will feel a connection with Nicklaus too—every single time you make a good swing, hit a good shot, and shoot a good score.

Index